THE LORD

THE LORD

The Portable New Century Edition

EMANUEL SWEDENBORG

Translated from the Latin by George F. Dole

SWEDENBORG FOUNDATION

West Chester, Pennsylvania

Originally published in Latin as *Doctrina Novae Hierosolymae de Domino,* Amsterdam, 1763.

Second printing, 2019
Third printing, with minor corrections, 2020

Printed in the United States of America

ISBN (library) 978-0-87785-503-3 (in *The Shorter Works of 1763*)
ISBN (e-book of library edition) 978-0-87785-707-5
ISBN (Portable) 978-0-87785-412-8
ISBN (e-book of Portable Edition) 978-0-87785-677-1

(The ISBN in the Library of Congress data shown below is the previous, 10-digit ISBN.)

Library of Congress Cataloging-in-Publication Data

Swedenborg, Emanuel, 1688-1772.
    [Doctrina Novae Hierosolymae de Domino. English]
    The Lord / Emanuel Swedenborg ; translated from the Latin by George F. Dole. — The Portable New Century Edition.
        pages cm
        ISBN 0-87785-412-2 (pbk.)
        1. New Jerusalem Church—Doctrines. 2. New Jerusalem Church—Controversial literature.
    I. Title.

BX8712.D92 2014

289'.4—dc23

                                                                        2014028849

Senior copy editor, Alicia L. Dole
Text designed by Joanna V. Hill
Ornaments from the first Latin edition, 1763
Typesetting by Alicia L. Dole
Cover designed by Karen Connor
Cover photograph by Magda Indigo

For information contact:
Swedenborg Foundation
320 North Church Street
West Chester, PA 19380 USA
Telephone: (610) 430-3222
Web: www.swedenborg.com
E-mail: info@swedenborg.com

Contents

Conventions Used in This Work   VII

The Lord

Preface   3

[1]   §§1–7 / The Entire Sacred Scripture Is about the Lord, and the Lord
Is the Word   5

[2]   §§8–11 / To Say That the Lord Fulfilled All of the Law Is to Say
That He Fulfilled All of the Word   21

[3]   §§12–14 / The Lord Came into the World to Subdue the Hells
and to Glorify His Human Nature; the Suffering on the Cross Was the
Last Battle by Which He Completely Defeated the Hells
and Completely Glorified His Human Nature   26

[4]   §§15–17 / The Lord Did Not Take Away Our Sins by His Suffering
on the Cross, but He Did Carry Them   32

[5]   §18 / The Imputation of the Lord's Merit Is Nothing More nor Less
Than the Forgiveness of Sins That Follows upon Repentance   38

[6]   §§19–28 / The Lord as the Divine-Human One Is Called "The Son
of God" and as the Word Is Called "The Son of Humanity"   41

[7]   §§29–36 / The Lord Made His Human Nature Divine
out of the Divine Nature within Himself, and in This Way
Became One with the Father   50

[8]   §§37–44 / The Lord Is God Himself, the Source and Subject
of the Word   68

[9]   §45 / God Is One, and the Lord Is God   78

[10]   §§46–54 / The Holy Spirit Is the Divine Nature That Emanates
from the Lord and Is the Lord Himself   79

[11]   §§55–61 / The Athanasian Statement of Faith Agrees with the Truth,
Provided That We Understand It to Be Referring Not to "a Trinity of
Persons" but to "a Trinity within One Person," Who Is the Lord   92

[12]   §§62–65 / The New Jerusalem in the Book of Revelation Means
       a New Church   99

Biographical Note   109

Conventions Used in This Work

MOST of the following conventions apply generally to the translations in the New Century Edition Portable series. For introductory material on the content and history of *The Lord*, and for annotations on the subject matter, with an extensive index, the reader is referred to the Deluxe New Century Edition volume *The Shorter Works of 1763*. In general, the introductions in this series discuss the key ideas presented in each work, as well as the relationship of those ideas to the history of ideas, and specifically to their eighteenth-century context. The subsequent influence of the works is also treated. The annotations provide definitions of unfamiliar terms; clarification of direct or indirect references to people, places, events, or other works; and information on matters that present challenges to current readers because of changes in culture over time.

Section numbers Following a practice common in his time, Swedenborg divided his published theological works into sections numbered in sequence from beginning to end. His original section numbers have been preserved in this edition; they appear in boxes in the outside margins. Traditionally, these sections have been referred to as "numbers" and designated by the abbreviation "n." In this edition, however, the more common section symbol (§) is used to designate the section numbers, and the sections are referred to as such.

Subsection numbers Because many sections throughout Swedenborg's works are too long for precise cross-referencing, Swedenborgian scholar John Faulkner Potts (1838–1923) further divided them into subsections; these have since become standard, though minor variations occur from one edition to another. These subsections are indicated by bracketed numbers that appear in the text itself: [2], [3], and so on. Because the beginning of the first *subsection* always coincides with the beginning of the *section* proper, it is not labeled in the text.

Citations of Swedenborg's text As is common in Swedenborgian studies, text citations of Swedenborg's works refer not to page numbers but to section numbers, which unlike page numbers are uniform in most editions. In citations the section symbol (§) is generally omitted after the title of a work by Swedenborg. Thus "*Heaven and Hell* 239" refers to section 239 (§239) of Swedenborg's *Heaven and Hell,* not to page 239 of any edition. Subsection numbers are given after a colon; a reference such as "239:2" indicates subsection 2 of section 239. The reference "239:1" would indicate the first subsection of section 239, though that subsection is not in fact labeled in the text. Where section numbers stand alone without titles, their function is indicated by the prefixed section symbol; for example, "§239:2".

Citations of the Bible Biblical citations in this edition follow the accepted standard: a semicolon is used between book references and between chapter references, and a comma between verse references. Therefore "Matthew 5:11, 12; 6:1; 10:41, 42; Luke 6:23, 35" refers to Matthew chapter 5, verses 11 and 12; Matthew chapter 6, verse 1; Matthew chapter 10, verses 41 and 42; and Luke chapter 6, verses 23 and 35. Swedenborg often incorporated the numbers of verses not actually represented in his text when listing verse numbers for a passage he quoted; these apparently constitute a kind of "see also" reference to other material he felt was relevant, and are generally retained in this edition without annotation. This edition also follows Swedenborg where he cites contiguous verses individually (for example, John 14:8, 9, 10, 11), rather than as a range (John 14:8–11). Occasionally this edition supplies a full, conventional Bible reference where Swedenborg omits one after a quotation.

Quotations in Swedenborg's works Some features of the original Latin text of *The Lord* have been modernized in this edition. For example, Swedenborg's first edition generally relies on context or italics rather than on quotation marks to indicate passages taken from the Bible or from other works. The manner in which these conventions are used in the original suggests that Swedenborg did not feel it necessary to belabor the distinction between direct quotation and paraphrase; neither did he mark his omissions from or changes to material he quoted, a practice in which this edition generally follows him. One exception consists of those instances in which Swedenborg did not include a complete sentence at the beginning or end of a Bible quotation. The omission in such cases has been marked in this edition with added points of ellipsis.

Italicized terms Any words in indented scriptural extracts that are here set in italics reflect a similar emphasis in the first edition.

Swedenborg's footnote The author's footnote to §64:1, indicated by a superscript letter *a* in the main body of the text, consists of cross-references to his previously published *Secrets of Heaven* (1749–1756).

Changes to and insertions in the text This translation is based on the first Latin edition, published by Swedenborg himself. It incorporates the silent correction of minor errors, not only in the text proper but in Bible verse references and in section references to Swedenborg's other published theological works. The text has also been changed without notice where the verse numbering of the Latin Bible cited by Swedenborg differs from that of modern English Bibles. Throughout the translation, references or cross-references that were implied but not stated have been inserted in square brackets []; for example, [John 3:27].

Chapter numbering Swedenborg did not number the chapters of *The Lord*. His decision not to do so seems to have been deliberate, and in accord with it chapter numbers are not included in the text. However, because some studies of his works make reference to chapter numbers, the table of contents provides them.

Biblical titles Swedenborg refers to the Hebrew Scriptures as the Old Testament and to the Greek Scriptures as the New Testament; his terminology has been adopted in this edition. As was the custom in his day, he refers to the Pentateuch (Genesis, Exodus, Leviticus, Numbers, and Deuteronomy) as the books of Moses, or simply as "Moses." Similarly, in sentences or phrases introducing quotations he sometimes refers to the Psalms as "David"; for example, in *The Lord* 33:5 he writes "There is also this in David," and then cites a passage from Psalm 24. Conventional references supplied in parentheses after such quotations specify their sources more precisely.

Problematic content Occasionally Swedenborg makes statements that, although mild by the standards of eighteenth-century theological discourse, now read as harsh, dismissive, or insensitive. The most problematic are assertions about or criticisms of various religious traditions and their adherents—including Judaism, ancient or contemporary; Roman Catholicism; Islam; and the Protestantism in which Swedenborg himself grew up. These statements are far outweighed in size and importance by other passages in Swedenborg's works earnestly maintaining the value of every individual and of all religions. This wider context is discussed in the introductions and annotations of the Deluxe Edition mentioned above. In the present format, however, problematic statements must be retained without comment. The other option—to omit them—would obscure some aspects of Swedenborg's presentation and in any case compromise its historicity.

Teachings
for the
New Jerusalem
on
the Lord

Preface

SOME years ago, I published five small works:

1. *Heaven and Hell*
2. *The New Jerusalem and Its Heavenly Teachings*
3. *Last Judgment*
4. *White Horse*
5. *Planets, or Earthlike Bodies, in the Universe*

Many things were presented in these works that had previously been unknown. Now the following works are to be offered to the public at the command of the Lord, who has been revealed to me.

Teachings for the New Jerusalem on the Lord
Teachings for the New Jerusalem on Sacred Scripture
Teachings about Life for the New Jerusalem: Drawn from the Ten Commandments
Teachings for the New Jerusalem on Faith
Supplements on the Last Judgment [and the Spiritual World]
Angelic Wisdom about Divine Providence
Angelic Wisdom about Divine Omnipotence, Omnipresence, Omniscience, Infinity, and Eternity
Angelic Wisdom about Divine Love and Wisdom
Angelic Wisdom about Life

"Teachings for the New Jerusalem" means teachings for the new church now to be established by the Lord. The fact is that the old church has come to its end, as can be seen from what is said in §§33–39 of the booklet *Last Judgment* and from more that will be said in the forthcoming booklets just listed.

The twenty-first chapter of Revelation tells us that after the judgment the New Jerusalem will come. As you will see under the last heading below [§§62–65], this New Jerusalem means a new church.

Teachings for the New Jerusalem on the Lord

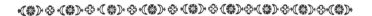

The Entire Sacred Scripture Is about the Lord, and the Lord Is the Word

WE read in John,

> In the beginning was the Word, and the Word was with God, and the Word was God. He was in the beginning with God. All things were made through him, and nothing that was made came about without him. In him there was life, and that life was the light for humankind. And the light shines in the darkness, but the darkness did not grasp it. And the Word became flesh and lived among us; and we saw his glory, glory like that of the only-begotten child of the Father. He was full of grace and truth. (John 1:1, 2, 3, 4, 5, 14)

In the same Gospel,

> Light has come into the world, but people loved darkness rather than light, because their deeds were evil. (John 3:19)

And elsewhere in the same Gospel,

> While you have the light, believe in the light, so that you may become children of the light. I have come into the world as a light so that anyone who believes in me will not remain in darkness. (John 12:36, 46)

We can see from this that the Lord is God from eternity and that he himself is that Lord who was born into the world. It actually says that the Word was with God and that the Word was God, as well as that nothing that was made came about without him, and then that the Word became flesh and that they saw him.

There is little understanding in the church of what it means to call the Lord "the Word." He is called the Word because the Word means divine truth or divine wisdom and the Lord is divine truth itself or divine wisdom itself. That is why he is also called the light that is said to have come into the world.

Since divine wisdom and divine love are one with each other and have been one in the Lord from eternity, it also says "in him there was life, and that life was the light for humankind." The life is divine love, and the light is divine wisdom.

This oneness is what is meant by saying both that "in the beginning the Word was with God" and that "the Word was God." "With God" is in God, since wisdom is in love and love is in wisdom. This is like the statement elsewhere in John, "Glorify me, Father, together with yourself, with the glory I had with you before the world existed" (John 17:5). "With yourself" is "in yourself." This is why it adds "and the Word was God." It says elsewhere that the Lord is in the Father and the Father is in him [John 14:10], and that the Father and he are one [John 10:30].

Since the Word is the divine wisdom of the divine love, it follows that it is Jehovah himself and therefore the Lord, the one by whom all things were made that were made, since everything was created out of divine love by means of divine wisdom.

2 We can see clearly that the specific Word meant here is the Word made known through Moses, the prophets, and the evangelists, since this is the actual divine truth from which angels get all their wisdom and from which we get our spiritual intelligence. In fact, angels in the heavens have the very same Word that we have in the world, though for us in the world it is earthly, while in the heavens it is spiritual. Further, since it is divine truth, the Word is also something divine that is emanating, and this is not only from the Lord but is the Lord himself.

Since it is the Lord himself, absolutely everything written in the Word is about the Lord alone. From Isaiah to Malachi every detail has to do with the Lord, either directly or in an opposite, negative sense.

No one has seen this before, but anyone who knows this and thinks of it can see it while reading, especially given the knowledge that in the Word there is not only an earthly meaning but a spiritual one as well; and that in this latter meaning the names of persons and places are used to mean something about the Lord and therefore something about heaven and the church that come from him—or something opposed to the Lord.

Since absolutely everything in the Word is about the Lord, and since the Word is the Lord because it is divine truth, we can see why it says "The Word became flesh and lived among us; and we saw his glory" [John 1:14]. We can also see why it says "While you have the light, believe in the light, so that you may become children of the light. I have come into the world as a light; anyone who believes in me will not remain in darkness" [John 12:36, 46]. "Light" is divine truth and therefore the Word.

For this reason, even nowadays anyone who turns to the Lord alone while reading the Word and who prays to him will find enlightenment in it.

I need at this point to say briefly what all the prophets of the Old Testament from Isaiah to Malachi have to say about the Lord, in general and in some detail. **3**

1. The Lord came into the world in the fullness of time [Galatians 4:4], which was when he was no longer recognized by Jews and when for this reason there was no longer anything left of the church; and unless the Lord had come into the world and revealed himself at that time, humankind would have suffered eternal death. He says in John, "If you do not believe that I am, you will die in your sins" (John 8:24).

2. The Lord came into the world to carry out a last judgment, thereby subduing the hells that were then in control, and doing so by means of battles or trials that were permitted to attack the human nature he had received from his mother, and by a constant succession of victories. If the hells had not been subdued, no one could have been saved.

3. The Lord came into the world to glorify his human nature—that is, to unite it to the divine nature that he had from conception.

4. The Lord came into the world to found a new church that would recognize him as Redeemer and Savior and that would be redeemed and saved through its love for and faith in him.

5. At the same time he was reorganizing heaven and uniting it with the church.

6. The suffering on the cross was the final battle or trial by means of which he completely subdued the hells and completely glorified his human nature.

In my forthcoming booklet on Sacred Scripture it will become evident that these are the sole subjects of the Word.

4 In support of this, I would like in this first chapter simply to cite passages from the Word where it says "that day," "on that day," or "at that time," passages where "day" and "time" mean the Lord's Coming. From Isaiah:

In *the days to come* it will happen that the mountain of Jehovah will be established as the highest of the mountains. On *that day* Jehovah alone will be exalted. *The day of Jehovah Sabaoth* is majestic and high above all. On *that day* people will throw away their idols of silver and gold. (Isaiah 2:2, 11, 12, 20)

On *that day* the Lord Jehovih will take away adornments. (Isaiah 3:18)

On *that day* the branch of Jehovah will be beautiful and glorious. (Isaiah 4:2)

[Their enemy] will roar against the people on *that day* and look down on the earth. Behold, there is darkness and anxiety, and the light will be growing darker among their ruins. (Isaiah 5:30)

It will happen on *that day* that Jehovah will whistle to the fly at the very end of the rivers of Egypt. On *that day* the Lord will shave [Judah] at the crossings of the river. On *that day* [a man] will bring [a young cow and two sheep] to life. On *that day* every place will become brambles and thorns. (Isaiah 7:18, 20, 21, 23)

What will you do on *the day* of visitation? Who will come? On *that day* Israel will rely on Jehovah, the Holy One of Israel, in truth. (Isaiah 10:3, 20)

It will happen on *that day* that the nations will seek out the root of Jesse, the one who stands as a sign for the peoples, and glory will be his rest. Above all, on *that day* the Lord will seek out the remnant of his people. (Isaiah 11:10, 11)

You will say on *that day,* "I will praise you, Jehovah." You will say on *that day,* "Praise Jehovah! Call upon his name!" (Isaiah 12:1, 4)

The day of Jehovah is near; it will come from Shaddai like destruction. Behold, *the cruel day of Jehovah* is coming—a day of resentment, blazing wrath, and anger. I will violently move heaven, and the earth will be shaken out of its place, on *the day* of his blazing anger. Its *time* is at hand and it will come, and the days will not be prolonged. (Isaiah 13:6, 9, 13, 22)

It will happen on *that day* that the glory of Jacob will be worn away. On *that day,* people will look back to their Maker, and their eyes [will look] toward the Holy One of Israel. On *that day* there will be cities of refuge in the forsaken parts of the forest. (Isaiah 17:4, 7, 9)

Those who dwell on [this] island will say on *that day,* "Look at what has happened to our hope!" (Isaiah 20:6)

On *that day* there will be five cities in the land of Egypt speaking the languages of Canaan. On *that day* there will be an altar to Jehovah in the center of Egypt. On *that day* there will be a highway from Egypt to Assyria, and Israel will be at the center of the land. (Isaiah 19:18, 19, 23, 24)

A day of tumult, trampling, and confusion from the Lord Jehovih Sabaoth . . . (Isaiah 22:5)

On *that day* Jehovah will punish the army of the high place and the monarchs of the earth. After a great many *days* they will be punished. Then the moon will blush and the sun will be ashamed. (Isaiah 24:21, 23)

It will be said on *that day,* "Behold, this is our God; we have waited for him to set us free." (Isaiah 25:9)

On *that day* this song will be sung in the land of Jehovah: "We have a strong city." (Isaiah 26:1)

On *that day* Jehovah will bring punishment with his sword. On *that day* answer him by saying, "A vineyard whose wine is pure." (Isaiah 27:1, 2, 12, 13)

On *that day* Jehovah Sabaoth will become an ornate crown and a diadem. (Isaiah 28:5)

Then on *that day* the deaf will hear the words of the book, and the eyes of the blind will see out of the darkness. (Isaiah 29:18)

On *the day* of the great slaughter, when the towers fall, there will be a channel of waters. The light of the moon will be like the light of the sun on *the day* when Jehovah binds up the breach of his people. (Isaiah 30:25, 26)

On *that day* they will each throw away their idols of silver and gold. (Isaiah 31:7)

The day of Jehovah's vengeance, *the year* of his recompense . . . (Isaiah 34:8)

These two things will come to you in one *day:* the loss of your children, and widowhood. (Isaiah 47:9)

My people will know my name, and on *that day* [they will know that] I am the one saying, "Here I am!" (Isaiah 52:6)

Jehovah has anointed me to proclaim *the year* of Jehovah's good pleasure and *the day* of vengeance for our God, to comfort all who are mourning. (Isaiah 61:1, 2)

The day of vengeance is in my heart and *the year* of my redeemed has arrived. (Isaiah 63:4)

From Jeremiah:

In *those days* you will no longer say, "The ark of the covenant of Jehovah." At that *time* they will call Jerusalem the throne of Jehovah. In *those days* the house of Judah will go to the house of Israel. (Jeremiah 3:16, 17, 18)

In *that day* the heart of the monarch will perish, and the heart of the royal family, and the priests and the prophets will be stunned. (Jeremiah 4:9)

Behold, *the days are coming* in which the earth will turn into a wasteland. (Jeremiah 7:32, 34)

They will fall among those who fall on *the day* of their visitation. (Jeremiah 8:12)

Behold, *the days are coming* in which I will execute judgment upon everyone whose foreskin has been circumcised. (Jeremiah 9:25)

In *the time* of their visitation they will perish. (Jeremiah 10:15)

There will be no remnant of them; I will bring evil upon them in *the year* of their visitation. (Jeremiah 11:23)

Behold, the *days are coming* in which it will no longer be said . . . (Jeremiah 16:14)

I will look at them in the back of the neck and not in the face on *the day* of their destruction. (Jeremiah 18:17)

Behold, *the days are coming* in which I will make this place a devastation. (Jeremiah 19:6)

Behold, *the days are coming* in which I will raise up for David a righteous branch who will rule as king. In *those days* Judah will be saved and Israel will dwell in safety. Therefore behold, *the days are coming* in which it will no longer be said . . . I will bring evil upon them in *the year* of their visitation. At the *very last of days* you will fully understand. (Jeremiah 23:5, 6, 7, 12, 20)

Behold, *the days are coming* in which I will turn back [the captivity of my people]. Alas, *that day* will be great, and there will be none like it. It will happen on *that day* that I will break the yoke and tear off the fetters. (Jeremiah 30:3, 7, 8)

The day will come when the guards cry out on Mount Ephraim, "Arise, let us climb Zion to Jehovah our God." Behold, *the days are coming* in which I will make a new covenant. *The days are coming* in which the city of Jehovah will be built. (Jeremiah 31:6, 27, 31, 38)

The days are coming in which I will perform the good word [that I promised]. In *those days* and at *that time* I will cause a righteous branch to grow for David. In *those days* Judah will be saved. (Jeremiah 33:14, 15, 16)

On *that day* I will bring words against this city for evil. You, though, I will rescue on *that day*. (Jeremiah 39:16, 17)

That day will be a *day* of vengeance for the Lord Jehovih Sabaoth; he will take vengeance on his enemies. *The day* of destruction has come upon them, *the time* of their visitation. (Jeremiah 46:10, 21)

Because of *the day that is coming* for devastation . . . (Jeremiah 47:4)

I will bring upon [Moab] *the year* of visitation. Nevertheless I will bring back its captives at *the very last of days.* (Jeremiah 48:44, 47)

I will bring destruction upon them at *the time* of their visitation. Their youths will fall in the streets and all their men of war will be cut down on *that day.* At *the very last of days* I will bring back their captives. (Jeremiah 49:8, 26, 39)

In *those days* and at *that time* the children of Israel and the children of Judah will come together and seek Jehovah their God. In *those days* and at *that time* the iniquity of Israel will be sought, but there will be none. Woe to [the Babylonians], because their *day* has come, the *time* of their visitation. (Jeremiah 50:4, 20, 27, 31)

They are vanity, a work of errors; they will perish at the *time* of their visitation. (Jeremiah 51:18)

From Ezekiel:

The end has come; the end has come. It has come upon you like the morning. The *time* has come; the *day* of tumult is near. Behold *the day;* see, it has come. The trunk has blossomed; violence has sprouted. *The day* has arrived; *the time* has come upon their whole multitude. Their silver and gold will not rescue them on *the day* of *Jehovah's* wrath. (Ezekiel 7:6, 7, 10, 12, 19)

People were saying of the prophet, "The vision that he is seeing will not happen for many days; his prophecy concerns *distant times.*" (Ezekiel 12:27)

They will not be able to stand up in the war on *the day* of Jehovah's wrath. (Ezekiel 13:5)

You pierced, godless prince of Israel, whose *day* has come, in *the time* of iniquity of the end . . . (Ezekiel 21:25, 29)

O city shedding blood in your own midst so that its *time* will come, you have made *the days* approach so that you will come to your years. (Ezekiel 22:3, 4)

Surely on *the day* that I take their strength from them, on *that day* someone who has been rescued will come to you with information for you to hear. On *that day* your mouth will be opened to speak with the one who has been rescued. (Ezekiel 24:25, 26, 27)

On *that day* I will cause the horn of the house of Israel to grow. (Ezekiel 29:21)

Wail "Alas for *the day,*" because *the day of Jehovah* is near, *the day of Jehovah* is near. It will be a *day* of cloud, *a time* for the nations. On *that day* messengers from me will go forth. (Ezekiel 30:2, 3, 9)

On *the day* you go down into hell . . . (Ezekiel 31:15)

I myself will search for my flock, [as] on *a day* when [a shepherd] is in the midst of [his] flock, and I will rescue them from all the places where they have been scattered on a cloudy and dark *day*. (Ezekiel 34:11, 12)

On *the day* when I cleanse you from all your iniquities . . . (Ezekiel 36:33)

Prophesy and say, "Will you not know it on *that day* when my people Israel settle safely? In *the days to come* I will bring you against my land, [This will happen] on *that day*, on *the day* when Gog comes upon the land [of Israel]. In my zeal, in *the day* of my indignation, surely on *this day* there will be a great earthquake upon the land of Israel," (Ezekiel 38:14, 16, 18, 19)

Behold, it is coming; *this* is *the day* of which I have spoken. It will happen on *that day* that I will give Gog a burial place in the land of Israel, so that the house of Israel will know that I, Jehovah, am their God from *that day* on. (Ezekiel 39:8, 11, 22)

From Daniel:

God in the heavens has revealed mysteries concerning what will happen in *the days to come*. (Daniel 2:28)

The time came for the saints to establish the kingdom. (Daniel 7:22)

"Understand that the vision concerns *the time of the end*." [Gabriel] said, "Behold, I am making known to you what will happen at *the end* of the wrath, because at the appointed *time the end* will come." The vision of evenings and mornings is the truth. Hide the vision, because it is for *many days*. (Daniel 8:17, 19, 26)

I have come to make you understand what will happen to your people at *the very last of days,* because the vision applies to days yet to come. (Daniel 10:14)

Those who understand will be tested in order to be purified and cleansed, until *the time of the end,* since it is yet for an appointed *time.* (Daniel 11:35)

At *that time* Michael will rise up, the great leader who stands up for the children of your people. There will be *a time* of distress such as there has not been since the nation [began]. At *this time,* however, your people will be rescued—everyone who is found written in the book. (Daniel 12:1)

You, Daniel, close up the words and seal the book until *the time of the end.* But from *the time* when the daily offering is taken away and the abomination that causes devastation is set up, there will be one thousand two hundred and ninety days. You will arise into your inheritance at *the end of days.* (Daniel 12:4, 9, 11, 13)

From Hosea:

I will make *an end* of the kingdom of the house of Israel. On *that day* I will break the bow of Israel. Great will be *the day* of Jezreel. (Hosea 1:4, 5, 11)

On *that day* you will call [me] "my husband." On *that day* I will make them a covenant. On *that day* I will respond. (Hosea 2:16, 18, 21)

The children of Israel will turn back and seek Jehovah their God and David their king at *the very last of days.* (Hosea 3:5)

Come, let us return to Jehovah. After two days he will revive us; on *the third day* he will raise us up, and we will live in his presence. (Hosea 6:1, 2)

The days of visitation have come; *the days* of retribution have come. (Hosea 9:7)

From Joel:

Alas for *the day,* because *the day* of Jehovah is at hand; it will come as destruction from Shaddai. (Joel 1:15)

The day of Jehovah is coming, *a day* of darkness and gloom, *a day* of clouds and thick darkness. Great is *the day of Jehovah* and extremely terrifying; who can endure it? (Joel 2:1, 2, 11)

Upon my male and female servants I will pour out my spirit in *those days*. The sun will be turned into darkness and the moon into blood before the great and terrifying *day of Jehovah* comes. (Joel 2:29, 31)

In *those days* and at *that time* I will gather all nations together. The *day of Jehovah* is at hand. On *that day* it will happen that the mountains will drip with new wine. (Joel 3:1, 2, 14, 18)

From Amos:

The strong of heart will flee naked on *that day*. (Amos 2:16)

On *the day* that I punish Israel for its sins . . . (Amos 3:14)

Woe to you who long for *the day of Jehovah*. What is *the day of Jehovah* to you? It will be a day of darkness and not of light. Surely *the day of Jehovah* will be a day of darkness and not of light, a day of thick darkness with no light at all. (Amos 5:18, 20)

The songs of the Temple will be howls on *that day*. On *that day* I will make the sun set at noon, and will darken the earth on a day of light. On *that day* beautiful young women and also young men will faint from thirst. (Amos 8:3, 9, 13)

On *that day* I will raise up the fallen tent of David. Behold, *the days are coming* when the mountains will drip with new wine. (Amos 9:11, 13)

From Obadiah:

On *that day* will I not destroy the wise of Edom? Do not rejoice over them on *the day* of their destruction, on *the day* of their distress. *The day* of Jehovah over all nations is at hand. (Obadiah verses 8, 12, 13, 14, 15)

From Micah:

On *that day* the lament will be "We have been utterly destroyed." (Micah 2:4)

At *the very last of days* the mountain of the house of Jehovah will be established on the top of the mountains. On *that day* I will gather the lame. (Micah 4:1, 6)

On *that day* I will cut off your horses and your chariots. (Micah 5:10)

The day of your watchmen, your visitation, has come. *The day* for building the walls is here. This is the *day* in which he will come to you. (Micah 7:4, 11, 12)

From Habakkuk:

The vision is still set for an appointed *time* and speaks concerning the end. If it delays, wait for it, because it will surely come and will not be postponed. (Habakkuk 2:3)

Jehovah, do your work in *the midst of the years;* in *the midst of the years* you will make it known. God will come. (Habakkuk 3:2)

From Zephaniah:

The *day of Jehovah* is at hand. On *the day* of the sacrifice of Jehovah I will execute judgment upon the royal family and upon the children of the monarch. On *that day* there will be the sound of shouting. At *that time* I will examine Jerusalem with lamps. The great *day of Jehovah* is at hand. *This day* is *a day* of blazing wrath; *a day* of distress and repression; *a day* of destruction and devastation; *a day* of darkness and gloom; *a day* of clouds and thick darkness; *a day* of trumpets and shouting. On *the day* of the blazing wrath of Jehovah the whole earth will be devoured and he will make a prompt end to all those who dwell in the land. (Zephaniah 1:7, 8, 10, 12, 14, 15, 16, 18)

. . . when *the day* of the wrath of Jehovah has not yet come upon us. Perhaps you may be hidden on *the day* of the wrath of Jehovah. (Zephaniah 2:2, 3)

Wait for me until *the day* I rise up for plunder, because that will be my judgment. On *that day* you will not be ashamed of your deeds. On *that day* it will be said to Jerusalem, "Do not be afraid." I will deal with your oppressors at *that time.* At *that time* I will bring you back. At *that time* I will gather you together to give you a name and praise. (Zephaniah 3:8, 11, 16, 19, 20)

From Zechariah:

I will remove the iniquity of that land in *one day.* On *that day* each of you will invite your neighbor under a vine and under a fig tree. (Zechariah 3:9, 10)

Then many nations will be joined to Jehovah on *that day.* (Zechariah 2:11)

In *those days* ten men will take hold of the hem of a man of Judah. (Zechariah 8:23)

Jehovah their God will save them on *that day,* as the flock of his people. (Zechariah 9:16)

My covenant was broken on *that day.* (Zechariah 11:11)

On *that day* I will make Jerusalem a heavy stone for all peoples. On *that day* I will strike every horse with confusion. On *that day* I will make the leaders of Judah like a fiery furnace surrounded by logs. On *that day* Jehovah will protect the inhabitants of Jerusalem. On *that day* I will seek to destroy all the nations [that are coming against Jerusalem]. On *that day* the mourning in Jerusalem will increase. (Zechariah 12:3, 4, 6, 8, 9, 11)

On *that day* a fountain will be opened for the house of David and for the inhabitants of Jerusalem. It will happen on *that day* that I will cut off the names of idols from the land. On *that day* the prophets will be ashamed. (Zechariah 13:1, 2, 4)

Behold, *the day of Jehovah* is coming. On *that day* his feet will stand on the Mount of Olives. On *that day* there will be no light or radiance. *One day* that will be known to Jehovah, not day or night, there will be light around the time of evening. On *that day* living waters will go forth from Jerusalem. On *that day* Jehovah will be one, and his name one. On *that day* there will be a great panic from Jehovah. On *that day* "Holiness belongs to Jehovah" will be engraved on the bells of the horses. There will no longer be a Canaanite in the house of Jehovah on *that day.* (Zechariah 14:1, 4, 6, 7, 8, 9, 13, 20, 21)

From Malachi:

Who can bear *the day* of his coming? Who will stand when he appears? They will be mine on *the day* that I make them my treasure. Behold, *the day* is coming, burning like an oven. Behold, I will send you Elijah the prophet before the great and terrifying *day of Jehovah* comes. (Malachi 3:2, 17; 4:1, 5)

From David:

In *his days* the righteous will flourish and there will be much peace, and he will reign from sea to sea, and from the river all the way to the ends of the earth. (Psalms 72:7, 8)

There are other instances elsewhere.

5   In these passages, *day* and *time* mean the Lord's Coming. *A day* or *time* of darkness, gloom, thick darkness, no light, devastation, the iniquity of the end, or destruction means the Lord's Coming, when he is no longer recognized and therefore when there is nothing left of the church.

A *day* that is cruel or terrifying, a *day* of blazing anger, wrath, panic, visitation, sacrifice, retribution, distress, war, or shouting means a coming of the Lord for judgment.

A *day* when Jehovah alone will be exalted, when he will be one and his name one, when the branch of Jehovah will be beautiful and glorious, when the righteous will flourish, when he will bring [a young cow and two sheep] to life, when he will search for his flock, when he will make a new covenant, when the mountains will drip with new wine, when living waters will go forth from Jerusalem, and when people will look back to the God of Israel (and many similar expressions) mean the Coming of the Lord to set up a new church that will recognize him as Redeemer and Savior.

6   Here I may add some passages that speak openly of the Lord's Coming, as follows:

> The Lord himself is giving you a sign. Behold, a virgin will conceive and bear a son, and she will call his name "*God with us.*" (Isaiah 7:14; Matthew 1:22, 23)

> A Child has been born to us; a Son has been given to us. Leadership will be upon his shoulder; and his name will be called Wonderful, Counselor, God, Hero, Father of Eternity, Prince of Peace. There will be no end of the increase of his leadership and peace, upon the throne of David and over his kingdom, to establish it in judgment and in justice from now on, even to eternity. (Isaiah 9:6, 7)

> A shoot will go forth from the trunk of Jesse, and a sprout from its roots will bear fruit. The spirit of Jehovah will rest upon him, a spirit of wisdom and intelligence, a spirit of counsel and strength. Justice will be a belt around his waist and truth a belt around his hips. Therefore it will happen on that day that the nations will seek the root of Jesse, the one who stands as a sign for the peoples, and glory will be his rest. (Isaiah 11:1, 2, 5, 10)

> Send the Lamb of the ruler of the earth from the rock by the wilderness to the mountain of the daughter of Zion. The throne has been

established through mercy; he sits upon it in truth in the tabernacle of David, judging and seeking a judgment, and hastening justice. (Isaiah 16:1, 5)

It will be said on that day, "Behold, this is our God; we have waited for him to set us free. *This is Jehovah; we have waited for him. Let us rejoice and be glad in his salvation.*" (Isaiah 25:9)

A voice of someone in the wilderness crying out, "Prepare a pathway for *Jehovah;* make level in the desert a highway for *our God.* The glory of *Jehovah* will be revealed, and all flesh will see it together." Behold, *the Lord Jehovih* is coming in strength, and his arm will rule for him. Behold, his reward is with him. Like a shepherd he will feed his flock. (Isaiah 40:3, 5, 10, 11)

My chosen one, in whom my soul has pleasure: I, *Jehovah,* have called you in righteousness. I will make you a covenant for the people, a light for the nations, to open blind eyes, and to lead the captives out of prison and those who are sitting in darkness out of the house of confinement. I am *Jehovah.* This is my name; I will not give my glory to another. (Isaiah 42:1, 6, 7, 8)

Who has believed our word and to whom has the arm of Jehovah been revealed? He has no form: we have seen him, but he has no beauty. He bore our diseases and carried our sorrows. (Isaiah 53:1–12)

"Who is this who is coming from Edom, with spattered garments from Bozrah, approaching in the immensity of his strength?" "I who speak justice and have the power to save, because the day of vengeance is in my heart and the year of my redeemed has arrived." Therefore he became their Savior. (Isaiah 63:1, 4, 8)

Behold, the days are coming in which I will raise up for David a righteous branch who will rule as king, and prosper, and bring about judgment and justice on earth. And this is his name: they will call him *"Jehovah our Righteousness."* (Jeremiah 23:5, 6; 33:15, 16)

Rejoice greatly, O daughter of Zion! Sound the trumpet, O daughter of Jerusalem! Behold, your king is coming to you. He is righteous and brings salvation. He will speak peace to the nations. His dominion will extend from sea to sea and from the river even to the ends of the earth. (Zechariah 9:9, 10)

Rejoice and be glad, O daughter of Zion! Behold, I am coming to dwell in your midst. Then many nations will be joined to *Jehovah* on that day and will become my people. (Zechariah 2:10, 11)

As for you, Bethlehem Ephrata, as little as you are among the thousands of Judah, one will come forth from you for me who will become the ruler in Israel; his coming forth is from ancient times, from the days of eternity. He will stand firm and feed [his flock] in the strength of *Jehovah*. (Micah 5:2, 4)

Behold, I am sending my angel, who will prepare the way before me; and *the Lord,* whom you seek, will suddenly come to his Temple, the angel of the covenant whom you desire. Behold, he is coming. But who can bear the day of his coming? Behold, I will send you Elijah the prophet before the great and terrifying day of Jehovah comes. (Malachi 3:1, 2; 4:5)

I was watching, and behold, someone like the Son of Humanity was coming with the clouds of the heavens. To him was given dominion and glory and a kingdom; and all peoples, nations, and tongues will worship him. His dominion is an everlasting dominion, one that will not pass away, and his kingdom is one that will not perish. All dominions will worship and obey him. (Daniel 7:13, 14, 27)

Seventy weeks have been allotted for your people and your holy city to put an end to sinning, to seal the vision and the prophet, and to anoint the Most Holy. Know then and understand: from [the time] the word goes forth that Jerusalem must be restored and built until [the time of] Messiah the Leader will be seven weeks. (Daniel 9:24, 25)

I will place his hand on the sea and his right hand on the rivers. He will cry out to me, "You are my Father, my God, and the Rock of my salvation." I will also make him the firstborn, high above the monarchs of the earth. I will make his seed endure to eternity and his throne as the days of the heavens. (Psalms 89:25, 26, 27, 29)

Jehovah said to my *Lord:* "Sit at my right until I make your enemies a stool for your feet. *Jehovah* will send the scepter of your strength from Zion, to rule in the midst of your enemies. You are a priest forever after the manner of Melchizedek." (Psalms 110:1, 2, 4; Matthew 22:44; Luke 20:42, 43)

"I have anointed [him as] my king over Zion, which is my holy mountain." "I will proclaim concerning the statute, '*Jehovah* has said to me, "You are my Son; today I have begotten you. I will make the nations your inheritance, the ends of the earth your possession."" Kiss the Son or he will become angry and you will perish on the way. Blessed are all who trust in him. (Psalms 2:6, 7, 8, 12)

You have indeed made him lack little in comparison with angels, and have crowned him with glory and honor. You have given him dominion over the works of your hands; you have placed all things under his feet. (Psalms 8:5, 6)

O *Jehovah*, be mindful of David, who swore to *Jehovah*, who vowed to the Mighty One of Jacob, "[God forbid] that I enter the tent of my home, go up to my bed, and grant sleep to my eyes, until I have found a place for *Jehovah*, a dwelling for the Mighty One of Jacob. Behold, we have heard of him in Ephrata; we have found him in the fields of the forest. We will enter his dwelling and bow down at the stool for his feet. Let your priests be clothed with justice, and let your saints rejoice." (Psalms 132:1–9)

But the passages cited here are only a few.

There will be ample demonstration that the whole Sacred Scripture is written about the Lord alone later, especially in what will be presented in the booklet on Sacred Scripture. This and this alone is why the Word is holy. It is also what is meant by the statement in Revelation that "The testimony of Jesus is the spirit of prophecy" (Revelation 19:10). **7**

To Say That the Lord Fulfilled All of the Law Is to Say That He Fulfilled All of the Word

MANY people nowadays believe that when it says of the Lord that he fulfilled the law [Matthew 5:17] it means that he fulfilled all of the Ten Commandments and that by doing so he became justice and justifies people in the world who believe this. **8**

That is not what it means, though. It means rather that he fulfilled everything that was written about him in the Law and the Prophets—that is, in the whole Sacred Scripture—because those writings, as stated under the preceding heading [§§1–7], are about him alone. The reason so many people believe something else is that they have not studied the Scriptures and seen what "the law" means in them.

In a strict sense "the law" does mean the Ten Commandments. In a broader sense it means everything Moses wrote in his five books; and in the broadest sense it means the whole Word.

It is common knowledge that *in a strict sense "the law" does mean the Ten Commandments.*

9 *In a broader sense "the Law" means everything Moses wrote in his five books,* as we can see from the following passages. In Luke,

> Abraham said to the rich man in hell, "They have *Moses and the prophets;* let them hear them. If they do not hear *Moses and the prophets,* they will not be persuaded even if someone rises from the dead." (Luke 16:29, 31)

In John,

> Philip said to Nathanael, "We have found the one of whom *Moses in the Law,* and also *the prophets,* wrote." (John 1:45)

In Matthew,

> Do not think that I have come to destroy *the Law and the Prophets:* I have come not to destroy but to fulfill. (Matthew 5:17, 18)

Or again,

> All *the Prophets and the Law* prophesied until John. (Matthew 11:13)

In Luke,

> *The Law and the Prophets* extended to [the time of] John; since then, the kingdom of God has been proclaimed. (Luke 16:16)

In Matthew,

> Whatever you want people to do for you, you do the same for them. This is *the Law and the Prophets.* (Matthew 7:12)

Or again,

> Jesus said, "You are to love the Lord your God with all your heart and with all your soul, and you are to love your neighbor as yourself. On these two commandments hang all *the Law and the Prophets.*" (Matthew 22:37, 39, 40)

In these passages "the Law and the Prophets" and "Moses and the prophets" mean everything written in the books of Moses and in the books of the prophets.

The following passages also show that "the Law" means specifically everything written by Moses. In Luke,

> When the days of their purification according to *the Law of Moses* were completed, they brought Jesus to Jerusalem to present him to the Lord—as it is written in *the Law of the Lord,* "Every male who opens the womb is to be called holy to the Lord,"—and to offer a sacrifice according to what is said in *the Law of the Lord,* "a pair of turtledoves or two young pigeons." And the parents brought Jesus into the Temple to do for him according to the custom of *the Law.* When they had completed all things according to *the Law of the Lord . . .* (Luke 2:22, 23, 24, 27, 39)

In John,

> *The Law of Moses* commanded that people like this should be stoned. (John 8:5)

Or again,

> *The Law* was given through Moses. (John 1:17)

We can see from these passages that sometimes it says "the Law" and sometimes "Moses" when it is talking about whatever is written in his books. See also Matthew 8:4; Mark 10:2, 3, 4; 12:19; Luke 20:28, 37; John 3:14; 7:19, 51; 8:17; 19:7.

Then too, many things that are commanded are called *the law* by Moses—for example, commandments about burnt offerings (Leviticus 6:9; 7:37), sacrifices (Leviticus 6:25; 7:1–11), the meal offering (Leviticus 6:14), leprosy (Leviticus 14:2), jealousy (Numbers 5:29, 30), and Naziritehood (Numbers 6:13, 21).

In fact, Moses himself called his books *the Law:*

> Moses wrote *this Law* and gave it to the priests, the sons of Levi, who carried the ark of the covenant of Jehovah, and said to them, "Take *the book* of this *Law* and put it beside the ark of the covenant of Jehovah." (Deuteronomy 31:9, 25, 26)

It was placed beside [the ark]: within the ark were the stone tablets that are "the law" in a strict sense.

Later, the books of Moses are called "the Book of the Law":

Hilkiah the high priest said to Shaphan the scribe, "I have found *the Book of the Law* in the house of Jehovah." When the king heard the words of *the Book of the Law,* he tore his clothes. (2 Kings 22:8, 11; 23:24)

10 *In the broadest sense, "the law" means everything in the Word,* as we can see from the following passages,

Jesus said, "Is it not written in *your law,* 'I said, "You are gods"?'" (John 10:34, in reference to Psalms 82:6)

The crowd replied, "We have heard from *the law* that the Christ will abide forever." (John 12:34, in reference to Psalms 89:29; 110:4; Daniel 7:14)

To fulfill the word written in *their law:* "They hated me for no reason." (John 15:25, in reference to Psalms 35:19)

The Pharisees said, "Have any of the leaders believed in him? Only this crowd, that does not know *the law.*" (John 7:48, 49)

It is easier for heaven and earth to pass away than for the tip of one letter of *the law* to fall. (Luke 16:17)

"The law" in these passages means the entire Sacred Scripture.

11 To say that the Lord fulfilled all of the law is to say that he fulfilled all of the Word, as we can see from passages where it says that the Scriptures were fulfilled by him and that everything was brought to completion. See, for example, the following.

Jesus went into the synagogue and stood up to read. He was handed the book of the prophet Isaiah. He unrolled the scroll and found the passage where it was written, "The spirit of the Lord is upon me, because he has anointed me to preach the gospel to the poor, to heal the brokenhearted, to proclaim release for the bound and sight for the blind, to preach the welcomed year of the Lord." Then he rolled up the scroll and said, "*Today this Scripture has been fulfilled* in your hearing." (Luke 4:16–21)

You search *the Scriptures,* and yet they testify of me. (John 5:39)

. . . that *the Scripture may be fulfilled,* "The one who eats bread with me has lifted up his heel against me." (John 13:18)

None of them is lost except the son of perdition, so that *the Scripture may be fulfilled.* (John 17:12)

. . . so that the word that he said would be fulfilled: "Of those whom you gave me I have lost none." (John 18:9)

Jesus said to Peter, "Put your sword in its place. How then *could the Scriptures be fulfilled,* that it must happen in this way? All this was done so that *the Scriptures of the prophets would be fulfilled."* (Matthew 26:52, 54, 56)

The Son of Humanity is going, as it has been written of him, so that *the Scriptures will be fulfilled.* (Mark 14:21, 49)

In this way *the Scripture was fulfilled* that said, "He was numbered with the transgressors." (Mark 15:28; Luke 22:37)

. . . so that *the Scripture would be fulfilled,* "They divided my garments among them, and for my tunic they cast lots." (John 19:24)

After this, Jesus, knowing that all things were now accomplished, so that *the Scriptures would be fulfilled . . .* (John 19:28)

When Jesus had received the vinegar, he said, *"It is finished,"* [that is, *fulfilled*]. (John 19:30)

These things were done so that *the Scripture would be fulfilled,* "Not one of his bones will be broken." And again, *another Scripture says,* "They will look on the one whom they pierced." (John 19:36, 37)

There are also other places where passages from the prophets are cited and it does not also say that the law or the Scripture has been fulfilled.

As for the whole Word having been written about him and his having come into the world to fulfill it, this is what he taught the disciples before he departed:

Jesus said to the disciples, "You are foolish, and you are slow of heart to believe everything the prophets said. Was it not necessary for the Christ to suffer this and enter into his glory?" Then beginning from *Moses and all the prophets,* he explained to them in *all the Scriptures the things concerning about himself.* (Luke 24:25, 26, 27)

Further,

Jesus said to the disciples, "These are the words that I spoke to you while I was still with you, that *all things must be fulfilled that were written in the Law of Moses and the Prophets and the Psalms concerning me."* (Luke 24:44, 45)

From these words of the Lord we can see that in the world he fulfilled all of the Word down to the smallest details:

> Truly, I tell you—until heaven and earth pass away, *not one little letter or the tip of one letter will pass from the law until all of it is fulfilled.* (Matthew 5:18)

From this we can now see clearly that to say that the Lord fulfilled all things of the law does not mean that he fulfilled all of the Ten Commandments but that he fulfilled all things of the Word.

The Lord Came into the World to Subdue the Hells and to Glorify His Human Nature; the Suffering on the Cross Was the Last Battle by Which He Completely Defeated the Hells and Completely Glorified His Human Nature

12 IT is common knowledge in the church that the Lord conquered death, which means hell, and that afterward he ascended into heaven in glory. What the church does not know, though, is that the Lord conquered death or hell by means of battles that are tests, and in so doing also glorified his human nature; and that his suffering on the cross was the last battle or trial by which he effected the conquest and glorification.

This is treated of in many passages in the prophets and David, but not so frequently in the Gospels. In the Gospels the trials that he was subject to from his childhood are summed up in his trials in the wilderness, with their concluding temptations by the Devil, and the final trials he suffered in Gethsemane and on the cross.

On his trials in the wilderness, which concluded with temptations by the Devil, see Matthew 4:1–11, Mark 1:12, 13, and Luke 4:1–13. By these,

however, are meant all his trials, even to the last. He did not disclose anything more about them to his disciples, for it says in Isaiah,

> He was oppressed, but did not open his mouth, like a lamb being led
> to slaughter. Like a sheep before its shearers he kept silence and did not
> open his mouth. (Isaiah 53:7)

On his trials in Gethsemane, see Matthew 26:36–44, Mark 14:32–41,
and Luke 22:39–46; and on his trials on the cross, see Matthew 27:33–56,
Mark 15:22–38, Luke 23:33–49, and John 19:17–37. Trials are nothing
more nor less than battles against the hells. On the trials or battles of
the Lord, see the booklet *The New Jerusalem and Its Heavenly Teachings*
(published in London) §§201, 302; and on trials in general, see §§189–
200 of the same work.

The Lord himself tells us in John that he completely defeated the
hells by his suffering on the cross:

> Now is the judgment of this world; *now the ruler of this world will be
> cast out.* (John 12:31)

The Lord said this when his suffering on the cross was at hand. And
again,

> *The ruler of this world* is judged. (John 16:11)

And again,

> Take heart! *I have overcome the world.* (John 16:33)

And in Luke,

> Jesus said, "I saw *Satan fall like lightning from heaven.*" (Luke 10:18)

The world, the ruler of this world, Satan, and the Devil mean hell.

The Lord tells us in John that he also completely glorified his human
nature by his suffering on the cross:

> After Judas went out, Jesus said, "Now *the Son of Humanity is glorified,
> and God is glorified* in him. If God is *glorified* in him, God will also *glo-
> rify* him in himself and glorify him immediately." (John 13:31, 32)

Again,

> Father, the hour has come. *Glorify* your Son, so that your Son may also
> *glorify* you. (John 17:1, 5)

And again,

> "Now my soul is troubled." And he said, "Father, *glorify* your name."
> And a voice came from heaven, saying, "I both have *glorified* it and will
> *glorify* it again." (John 12:27, 28)

In Luke,

> Was it not necessary for Christ to suffer this and enter into his *glory?*
> (Luke 24:26)

These sayings were about his suffering. Glorification is the complete union
of the divine nature and the human nature, so it says "God will also glorify
him in himself."

14   There are many passages in the prophets where it is foretold that the
Lord would come into the world to bring everything in the heavens and
on earth back into order, that he would accomplish this by battles against
the hells that were then attacking everyone coming into the world and
leaving the world, and that in this way he would become justice and save
people who could not be saved otherwise. I will cite only a few. [2] In
Isaiah:

> "Who is this who is coming from Edom, with spattered garments from
> Bozrah, noble in his clothing, and approaching in the immensity of
> his strength?" "I who speak justice and have the power to save." "Why
> are your garments red? Why are your garments like those of someone
> who is treading a winepress?" "I have trodden the winepress alone,
> and there has been no man of the people with me. Therefore I have
> trodden them in my wrath and trampled them in my blazing anger.
> Victory over them is spattered on my garments, because the day of
> vengeance is in my heart and the year of my redeemed has arrived. My
> own arm brought about salvation for me; I have driven their victory
> down into the earth." He said, "Behold, these are my people, my chil-
> dren." Therefore he became their Savior. Because of his love and his
> mercy he has redeemed them. (Isaiah 63:1–9)

This is about the Lord's battles against the hells. The clothing in which
he was noble and which was red means the Word, which had suffered
violence at the hands of the Jewish people. The actual battles against the
hells and victory over them is described by his treading them in his
wrath and trampling them in his blazing anger. His having fought alone
and from his own power is described by "There has been no man of the

people with me; my own arm has brought about salvation for me; I have driven their victory down into the earth." His having brought about salvation and redemption by this is described by "Therefore he became their Savior; because of his love and his mercy he redeemed them." The fact that this was the reason for his Coming is described by "The day of vengeance is in my heart and the year of my redeemed has arrived." [3] In Isaiah,

> He saw that there was no one and was amazed that no one was interceding. Therefore his own arm brought about salvation for him and his own justice sustained him. Therefore he put on justice like a breastplate and put a helmet of salvation on his head. He also put on garments of vengeance and wrapped himself in zeal like a cloak. Then he came to Zion as the Redeemer. (Isaiah 59:16, 17, 20)

This too is about the Lord's battles with the hells while he was in the world. His fighting against them alone, with his own strength, is meant by "He saw that there was no one. Therefore his own arm brought about salvation"; his thereby becoming justice is meant by "his own justice sustained him. Therefore he put on justice like a breastplate"; and his bringing about redemption in this way is meant by "Then he came to Zion as the Redeemer." [4] In Jeremiah,

> They were terrified. Their mighty ones were beaten down. They fled in flight and did not look back. That day is a day of vengeance for the Lord Jehovih Sabaoth, to take vengeance on his enemies. The sword will devour and be satisfied. (Jeremiah 46:5, 10)

The Lord's battle with the hells and victory over them are described by "They were terrified. They fled in flight and did not look back." Their mighty ones and the enemies are the hells, because everyone in hell harbors hatred toward the Lord. His coming into the world for this reason is meant by "That day is a day of vengeance for the Lord Jehovih Sabaoth, to take vengeance on his enemies." [5] In Jeremiah,

> Their youths will fall in the streets and all their men of war will be cut down on that day. (Jeremiah 49:26)

In Joel,

> Jehovah puts forth his voice before his army. Great is the day of Jehovah, and extremely terrifying; who can endure it? (Joel 2:11)

In Zephaniah,

> On the day of Jehovah's sacrifice I will execute judgment upon the royal family, upon the children of the monarch, and upon all who dress themselves in foreign clothing. This day is a day of distress, a day of trumpets and shouting. (Zephaniah 1:8, 15, 16)

In Zechariah,

> Jehovah will go forth and fight against the nations like the day that he fought on the day of battle. On that day his feet will stand on the Mount of Olives, which faces Jerusalem. Then you will flee into the valley of my mountains. On that day there will be no light or radiance. Jehovah, though, will become king over all the earth. On that day Jehovah will be one, and his name one. (Zechariah 14:3, 4, 5, 6, 9)

In these passages too we are dealing with the Lord's battles. "That day" means his Coming; "the Mount of Olives, which faces Jerusalem" was where the Lord stayed by himself—see Mark 13:3, 4; 14:26; Luke 21:37; 22:39; John 8:1; and elsewhere. [6] In David,

> The cords of death surrounded me; the cords of hell surrounded me; the snares of death confronted me. Therefore he sent forth arrows and many bolts of lightning, and confounded them. I will pursue my enemies and seize them, and I will not turn back until I have devoured them. I will strike them down so that they cannot rise up again. You will gird me with strength for war and put my enemies to flight. I will crush them like dust before the face of the wind; I will empty them out like the mire of the streets. (Psalms 18:4, 14, 37, 39, 40, 42)

The cords and snares of death that surrounded and confronted him mean trials that are also called cords of hell because they come from hell. These verses and the rest of the whole psalm are about the Lord's battles and victories, which is why it also says, "You will make me the head of the nations; people I have not known will serve me" (verse 43). [7] In David,

> Gird a sword on your thigh, mighty one. Your arrows are sharp; peoples will fall beneath you, those who are the king's enemies at heart. Your throne is for the ages and forever. You have loved justice; therefore God has anointed you. (Psalms 45:3, 5, 6, 7)

This too is about battling with the hells and bringing them under control, since the whole psalm is talking about the Lord—specifically, his battles, his glorification, and his salvation of the faithful. In David,

> Fire will go forth before him; it will burn up his enemies round about; the earth will see and fear. The mountains will melt like wax before the Lord of the whole earth. The heavens will proclaim his justice, and all the peoples will see his glory. (Psalms 97:3, 4, 5, 6)

This psalm similarly is dealing with the Lord and with the same issues. [8] In David,

> Jehovah said to my Lord, "Sit at my right until I make your enemies a stool for your feet, to rule in the midst of your enemies." The Lord is on your right; on the day of his wrath he has struck down monarchs. He has filled [the nations] with corpses; he has struck the head of a great land. (Psalms 110:1, 5, 6)

Some words of the Lord himself show that these things were spoken about the Lord: see Matthew 22:44, Mark 12:36, and Luke 20:42. Sitting at the right means omnipotence, the enemies mean the hells, monarchs mean people there who have evil lives and false beliefs. Making them a stool for his feet, striking them down on the day of wrath, and filling [the nations] with corpses mean destroying their power; and striking the head of a great land means destroying all of their power.

[9] Since the Lord alone overcame the hells with no help from any angel, he is called *Hero and Man of War* (Isaiah 42:13), *King of Glory, Jehovah the Mighty, Hero of War* (Psalms 24:8, 10), *the Mighty One of Jacob* (Psalms 132:2, 5), and in many passages *Jehovah Sabaoth*, that is, Jehovah of Armies of War.

Then too, his Coming is called *the day of Jehovah*—terrifying, cruel, a day of resentment, blazing anger, wrath, vengeance, destruction, war, trumpet, shouting, and panic, as we can see from the passages cited in §4 above.

[10] Since a last judgment was carried out by the Lord when he was in the world, by battling with the hells and bringing them under control, in many passages it speaks of a *judgment* that is going to be executed. See David, for example—"Jehovah is coming to judge the earth; he will judge the world with justice and the peoples with truth" (Psalms 96:13)—and frequently elsewhere.

These citations are from the prophetic books of the Word.

[11] In the historical books of the Word, though, matters of the same sort are represented as wars between the children of Israel and various nations. This is because everything in the Word, whether prophetical or historical, is written about the Lord. So the Word is divine when it tells of the rituals of the Israelite church; for example, there are many secrets concerning the Lord's glorification contained in the descriptions of burnt offerings and sacrifices, in the Sabbaths and festivals, and in the priesthood of Aaron and the Levites. The same holds true for other parts of the books of Moses, the material called laws, judgments, and statutes. This is also the intent of what the Lord said to the disciples—that it was fitting for him to fulfill everything written about him in the Law of Moses (Luke 24:44); and what he said to the Jews—that Moses had written about him (John 5:46).

[12] We can now see from this that the Lord came into the world to subdue the hells and to glorify his human nature, and that the suffering on the cross was the last battle, by which he completely defeated the hells and completely glorified his human nature.

You may find more on this subject, though, in the forthcoming booklet *Sacred Scripture* [§103], where there is a complete collection in one place of all the passages in the prophetic Word that deal with the Lord's battles against the hells and victories over them, or (which amounts to the same thing) with the last judgment that he executed when he was in the world, together with the passages about his suffering and the glorification of his human nature. Of these latter there are so many that if they were fully quoted, they would fill volumes.

The Lord Did Not Take Away Our Sins by His Suffering on the Cross, but He Did Carry Them

15 THERE are people in the church who believe that through his suffering on the cross the Lord took away our sins and made satisfaction to the Father, and by so doing brought about redemption. Others believe that he transferred to himself the sins of those who have faith in him, carried those sins, and cast them into the depths of the sea—that is, into hell. They support this among themselves by what John says of Jesus,

> Behold the Lamb of God, who is taking up the sins of the world. (John 1:29)

and by the Lord's words in Isaiah,

> He bore our diseases and carried our sorrows. He was pierced because of our transgressions and bruised because of our iniquities. Chastisement was upon him for the sake of our peace; with his wound, healing was given to us. Jehovah made the iniquities of us all fall upon him. He was oppressed and afflicted, but did not open his mouth, like a lamb being led to slaughter. He was cut off from the land of the living. He suffered a blow because of the transgression of my people, to send the ungodly to their grave and the rich to their deaths. As a result of the labor of his soul, he will see and be satisfied. By means of his knowledge he will justify many, because he himself carried their iniquities. He emptied out his own soul even to death and was counted among transgressors. He bore the sins of many and interceded for transgressors. (Isaiah 53:3–end)

Both of these passages are talking about the Lord's trials and suffering; his taking up our sins, [bearing] our diseases, and having the iniquities of us all fall upon him mean something similar to his carrying our sorrows and our iniquities.

[2] So I need to say first of all what his carrying iniquities means and then what his taking them up means. The true meaning of his carrying iniquities is that he was subjected to severe trials and endured being treated by the Jews the way the Word was treated by them; and they dealt with him in that way precisely because he was the Word. The church among the Jews was in utter shambles at that time; it had been brought to ruin by their perversion of everything in the Word to the point that there was nothing true left. As a result, they did not recognize the Lord. That is in fact the intent and meaning behind each detail of the Lord's suffering.

The prophets suffered in much the same way because they represented the Lord's Word and therefore his church, and the Lord was the quintessential prophet.

[3] We can tell that the Lord was the quintessential prophet from the following passages:

Jesus said, "*A prophet* is not without honor except in his own country and in his own house." (Matthew 13:57; Mark 6:4; Luke 4:24)

Jesus said, "It is not fitting for *a prophet* to die outside of Jerusalem." (Luke 13:33)

They said of Jesus, "He is *a prophet* from Nazareth." (Matthew 21:11; John 7:40, 41)

Fear came upon all, and they glorified God, saying that *a great prophet* had been raised up among them. (Luke 7:16)

A prophet will be raised up from among his people; they will obey his words. (Deuteronomy 18:15–19)

[4] We can tell from the following passages that much the same was done to the prophets.

The prophet Isaiah was commanded to represent the state of the church by taking the sackcloth off his waist and the sandals off his feet and going naked and barefoot for three years as a sign and a wonder (Isaiah 20:2, 3).

The prophet Jeremiah was commanded to represent the state of the church by buying a belt and putting it around his waist without putting it in water, then hiding it in a crevice in the rocks near the Euphrates; after some days he found it ruined (Jeremiah 13:1–7).

The same prophet represented the state of the church by not taking a wife for himself in that place or entering the house of mourning or going out to grieve or going into the banquet house (Jeremiah 16:2, 5, 8).

[5] The prophet Ezekiel was commanded to represent the state of the church by taking a barber's razor to his head and his beard and then dividing the hair, burning a third of it in the middle of the city, striking a third with a sword, and scattering a third to the wind; also, he was told to bind a few hairs in his hems and eventually to throw a few into the midst of a fire and burn them (Ezekiel 5:1–4).

The same prophet was commanded to represent the state of the church by packing his belongings to take into exile and traveling to another place in the sight of the children of Israel. In a while he was to take out his belongings and leave in the evening through a hole dug through the wall, covering his face so that he could not see the ground. And this was to be a sign to the house of Israel. The prophet was also to say, "Behold, I am a sign for you: what I have done, [your leaders] will do" (Ezekiel 12:3–7, 11).

[6] The prophet Hosea was commanded to represent the state of the church by taking a whore as his wife. He did so, and she bore him three children, the first of whom he named Jezreel, the second No Mercy, and the third Not My People (Hosea 1:2–9).

Another time he was commanded to go love a woman who had a lover but was also committing adultery; he bought her for fifteen pieces of silver (Hosea 3:1, 2).

[7] The prophet Ezekiel was commanded to represent the state of the church by taking a clay tablet, carving Jerusalem on it, laying siege to it, building a siege wall and a mound against it, putting an iron plate between himself and the city, and lying on his left side for three hundred ninety days and then on his right side [for forty days]. He was also told to take wheat, barley, lentils, millet, and spelt and make himself bread from them, which he was then to weigh and eat. He was also told to bake a cake of barley over human dung; and because he begged not to do this, he was commanded to bake it over cow dung instead (Ezekiel 4:1–15).

Further, prophets also represented other things—Zedekiah with the horns of iron that he made, for example (1 Kings 22:11). Then there was another prophet who was struck and wounded and who put ashes over his eyes (1 Kings 20:37, 38).

[8] In general, prophets used a robe of coarse hair (Zechariah 13:4) to represent the Word in its outermost meaning, which is the literal meaning; so Elijah wore that kind of robe and had a leather belt around his waist (2 Kings 1:8). Much the same is true of John the Baptist, who had clothing of camels' hair and a leather belt around his waist, and who ate locusts and wild honey (Matthew 3:4).

We can see from this that the prophets represented the state of the church and the Word. In fact, anyone who represents one represents the other as well because the church is from the Word, and its life and faith depend on its acceptance of the Word. So too, wherever prophets are mentioned in both Testaments it means the body of teaching the church draws from the Word, while the Lord as the supreme prophet means the church itself and the Word itself.

The state of the church in relation to the Word, as represented by the **16** prophets, was the meaning of their "carrying the iniquities and sins of the people." This we can see from what is said about the prophet Isaiah, that he went naked and barefoot for three years as a sign and a wonder

(Isaiah 20:3). It says of Ezekiel that he was to take out his belongings to go into exile and cover his face so that he could not see the ground, and that this was to be a sign to the house of Israel; and he was also to say, "I am a sign for you" (Ezekiel 12:6, 11).

[2] It is abundantly clear from Ezekiel that this was carrying the people's iniquities, when Ezekiel was commanded to lie on his left side for three hundred ninety days and on his right side for forty days against Jerusalem and to eat a cake of barley baked over cow dung. We read there,

> Lie on your left side and place *the iniquity of the house of Israel* on it. According to the number of days that you lie on it *you will carry* their *iniquity*. I will give you years of their iniquity matching the number of days, three hundred ninety days, so that *you carry the iniquity of the house of Israel*. When you have finished them, you will lie a second time, but on your right side for forty days *to carry the iniquity of the house of Judah*. (Ezekiel 4:4, 5, 6)

[3] By carrying the iniquities of the house of Israel and the house of Judah in this way, the prophet did not take them away and thus atone for them, but simply represented them and made them clear. This we can see from what follows:

> Thus says Jehovah: "The children of Israel will eat their bread defiled among the nations where I am going to send them. Behold, I am breaking the staff of bread in Jerusalem so that they will lack bread and water. They will all become desolate and waste away because of their iniquity." (Ezekiel 4:13, 16, 17)

[4] Similarly, when Ezekiel appeared in public and said, "Behold, I am a sign for you," he also said, "What I have done, [your leaders] will do" (Ezekiel 12:6, 11).

Much the same is meant, then, when it says of the Lord, "He bore our diseases and carried our sorrows. Jehovah made the iniquities of us all fall upon him. By means of his knowledge he justified many, because he himself carried their iniquities." This is from Isaiah 53:[4, 6, 11], where the whole chapter is about the Lord's suffering.

[5] We can see from the details of the narrative of his suffering that he, as the greatest prophet, represented the state of the church in its relationship to the Word. For example, he was betrayed by Judas; he was seized and condemned by the chief priests and elders; they struck him with their fists; they struck his head with a stick; they put a crown of thorns on him; they divided his garments and cast lots on his tunic; they

crucified him; they gave him vinegar to drink; they pierced his side; he was entombed; and on the third day he rose again [Matthew 26:14–16, 47–68; 27:1–61; 28:1–10; Mark 14:43–65; 15:15–37; 16:1–8; Luke 22:47–71; 23:26–56; 24:1–35; John 18:1–14; 19:1–30; 20:1–18].

[6] His being betrayed by Judas meant that this was being done by the Jewish people, who at that time were custodians of the Word, since Judas represented them. His being seized and condemned by the chief priests and elders meant that this was being done by the whole church. Their whipping him, spitting in his face, striking him with their fists, and striking his head with a stick meant that they were doing this kind of thing to the Word in regard to its divine truths, all of which are about the Lord. Their putting a crown of thorns on him meant that they falsified and contaminated these truths. Their dividing his garments and casting lots on his tunic meant that they destroyed the connectedness of all the truths of the Word—though not its spiritual meaning, which is symbolized by the tunic. Their crucifying him meant that they destroyed and profaned the whole Word. Their giving him vinegar to drink meant offering nothing but things that were distorted and false, which is why he did not drink it and then said, "It is finished." Their piercing his side meant that they completely stifled everything true in the Word and everything good in it. His entombment meant his putting off any residual human nature from his mother. His rising again on the third day meant his glorification. Much the same is meant by the passages in the prophets and David where these events were foretold.

[7] That is why, after he had been whipped and led out wearing the crown of thorns and the purple robe the soldiers had put on him, he said, "Behold the man" (John 19:1–5). This was said because a human being means a church, since "the Son of Humanity" means what is true in the church, therefore the Word.

We can see from all this that his "carrying iniquities" means that he represented and offered an image of the sins that were being committed against the divine truths of the Word. And we will see in the following pages [§§19–29] that the Lord endured and suffered these torments as the Son of Humanity and not as the Son of God. "The Son of Humanity" means the Lord as the Word.

I need now to say something about the meaning of the Lord's "taking up sins" [John 1:29]. His "taking up sins" means much the same as his redeeming us and saving us, since the Lord came into the world so that we could be saved; if he had not come no one could have been reformed and reborn and therefore saved. This could happen, though, **17** after the Lord had taken all power away from the Devil—that is, from hell—and had glorified his human nature—that is, united it to the divine nature of his Father. If these things had not happened, no human beings could have accepted anything divinely true that dwelt within them, let alone anything divinely good, because the Devil, who had had the greater power before these events, would have snatched it from their hearts.

[2] We can see from all this that the Lord did not take away sins by his suffering on the cross, but that he does take away sins—that is, lay them aside—in those who believe in him and live by his commandments. This is what the Lord is telling us in Matthew:

> Do not think that I have come to destroy the Law and the Prophets. Whoever breaks the least of these commandments and teaches others to do the same will be called the least in the kingdom of the heavens; but whoever does and teaches [these commandments] will be called great in the kingdom of the heavens. (Matthew 5:17, 19)

[3] Reason alone should convince anyone who is the least bit enlightened that sins can be taken away from us only by active repentance—that is, by our seeing our sins, begging the Lord for help, and desisting from them. To see and believe and teach anything else does not come from the Word or from sound reason but from the desire and ill intent that come from our own sense of self-importance—an attitude that corrupts our understanding.

The Imputation of the Lord's Merit Is Nothing More nor Less Than the Forgiveness of Sins That Follows upon Repentance

18 IT is believed in the church that the Lord was sent by the Father to make atonement for the human race, and that this was accomplished by his fulfilling the law and by his suffering on the cross, that in this way he bore our damnation and made satisfaction, and that if it were not for this atonement, satisfaction, and propitiation, the human race would have died an eternal death. This is believed to have been a matter of justice, and some even refer to it as retributive.

It is quite true that we would all have perished if the Lord had not come into the world, but how we should understand the Lord's fulfilling everything in the law has been explained in its own chapter above [§§8–11]. An explanation of why he suffered the cross has also been given in its own treatment [§§12–14, 15–17], enabling us to see that this was not a matter of retributive justice, since that is not a divine attribute. Justice, love, mercy, and goodness are divine attributes, and God is justice itself, love itself, mercy itself, and goodness itself. Further, where we find these we find no vindictiveness and therefore no retributive justice.

[2] Until now, many people have understood "the fulfilling of the law" and "the suffering on the cross" as the two means by which the Lord made satisfaction for the human race and delivered it from the predicted or fated damnation. If we believe that these two actions—which constituted the Lord's merit—made satisfaction for us, and we put this together with the principle that we are saved simply by believing that they happened, what follows is the dogma that the Lord's merit is imputed to us. However, this dogma collapses in the light of what has been said about the Lord's fulfillment of the law and his suffering on the cross. At the same time we can see that "the imputation of merit" is a phrase without substance unless we take it to mean the forgiveness of sins that follows repentance. You see, nothing that belongs to the Lord can be credited to us, but salvation can be transferred to us by the Lord after we practice repentance—that is, after we see and acknowledge our sins and then desist from them, doing this because of the Lord. Then there is a way in which salvation is transferred to us: we are saved not on the basis of our own worth and our own righteousness but by the Lord, the only one who has fought and overcome the hells and who alone thereafter fights for us and overcomes the hells for us. [3] These accomplishments are the Lord's merit and righteousness, and they can never be credited to our account—because if they were, the Lord's merit and righteousness would be attributed to us as though they were our own. This is something that never happens and that cannot happen. If imputation were possible, we could claim the Lord's merit when we were impenitent and irreverent and think ourselves justified by doing so. Yet this would be polluting what is holy with profane things and profaning the Lord's name, because it would be focusing

our thoughts on the Lord but our will on hell, when in fact all we are is what our will intends.

There is a faith that is God's and a faith that is our own. People who practice repentance have the faith that is God's. People who do not practice repentance but think in terms of imputation have a faith that is their own. God's faith is a living faith; our own faith is a dead faith.

[4] The following passages show that both the Lord himself and his disciples taught repentance and the forgiveness of sins.

> Jesus began to preach and to say, "*Repent,* because the kingdom of the heavens is at hand." (Matthew 4:17)

> Jesus said, "Bear fruit that is consistent with *repentance.* The axe is already lying against the root of the trees. Every tree that does not bear good fruit is cut down and thrown into the fire." (Luke 3:8, 9)

> Jesus said, "Unless you *repent,* you will all perish." (Luke 13:3, 5)

> Jesus came preaching the gospel of the kingdom of God, saying, "The time is fulfilled, and the kingdom of God is at hand. *Repent,* and believe in the gospel." (Mark 1:14, 15)

> Jesus sent out his disciples, and they went out and preached that people should *repent.* (Mark 6:12)

> Jesus said to the apostles that it was necessary for them to preach *repentance and the forgiveness of sins* in his name to all nations, beginning at Jerusalem. (Luke 24:47)

> John preached a baptism of *repentance for the forgiveness of sins.* (Luke 3:3; Mark 1:4)

"Baptism" means a spiritual washing, which is a washing from sins and is called "rebirth."

[5] This is how the Lord describes repentance and the forgiveness of sins in John:

> He came to what was his own, and yet his own people did not accept him. But as many as did accept him, he gave them power to become children of God and believe in his name, who were born, not of blood, and not of the will of the flesh, and not of the will of a man, but of God. (John 1:11, 12, 13)

"His own people" means people of the church at that time, the church where the Word was; "children of God" and "believing in his name" mean people who believe in the Lord and who believe in the Word; blood means distortions of the Word and justifying what is false by that means; the will of the flesh means the will belonging to our own [lower] self, which is essentially evil; the will of a man means the understanding belonging to our own [lower] self, which is essentially false; and "those born of God" means people who have been reborn by the Lord.

We can see from this that we are saved if we are focused on good and loving actions that come from the Lord and on truths of our faith that come from the Lord; we are not saved if we are wrapped up in ourselves.

The Lord as the Divine-Human One Is Called "The Son of God" and as the Word Is Called "The Son of Humanity"

THE church is convinced that the Son of God is the second person of the Godhead, distinct from the person of the Father, which results in a belief in a Son of God born from eternity. Since this is everywhere accepted and is about God, there is neither ability nor permission to think about this matter at all intelligently, not even about what it means to be "born from eternity." This is because people who think about it intelligently inevitably find themselves saying, "This is completely beyond me. Still, I say it because everybody else says it, and I believe it because everybody else believes it." They should realize, though, that there is no Son from eternity; rather, the Lord is from eternity. Only when they realize what "the Lord" means and what "the Son" means can they think intelligently about a triune God.

[2] As for the fact that the Lord's human side—conceived by Jehovah the Father and born of the Virgin Mary—was the Son of God, this is obvious from the following in Luke:

> The angel Gabriel was sent by God to a city in Galilee named Nazareth, to a virgin betrothed to a man whose name was Joseph, from the

house of David. The virgin's name was Mary. Having come in, the angel said to her, "Greetings, you who have attained grace. The Lord is with you; you are blessed among women." When she saw him, she was troubled by what he said and considered what kind of salutation this was. The angel said to her, "Do not be afraid, Mary: you have found favor with God. Behold, you will conceive and bear a Son, and you will call his name Jesus. He will be great and will be called *the Son of the Highest*." But Mary said to the angel, "How will this take place, since I have not had intercourse?" The angel replied and said to her, "*The Holy Spirit will descend upon you,* and *the power of the Highest will cover you;* therefore the *Holy One* that is born from you will be called *the Son of God*." (Luke 1:26–35)

This passage says "you will conceive and bear a Son. He will be great and will be called the Son of the Highest," and again, "The Holy One that is born from you will be called the Son of God." We can see from this that it is the human nature conceived by God and born of the Virgin Mary that is called "the Son of God." [3] In Isaiah,

The Lord himself is giving you a sign. Behold, a virgin will conceive and bear a *son,* and she will call his name "*God with us*." (Isaiah 7:14)

We can see that the Son born of the Virgin and conceived by God is the one who will be called "God with us" and is therefore the one who is the Son of God. There is further support for this in Matthew 1:22, 23. [4] In Isaiah:

A *Child* has been born to us; a *Son* has been given to us. Leadership is upon his shoulder; and his name will be called Wonderful, Counselor, God, Hero, *Father of Eternity,* Prince of Peace. (Isaiah 9:6)

It is the same here, since it says "A Child has been born to us; a Son has been given to us," who is not a Son from eternity but a Son born into the world. We can see this also from what the prophet says in verse 6 there and from the words of the angel Gabriel to Mary (Luke 1:32, 33), which are similar. [5] In David:

"I will proclaim concerning the statute, 'Jehovah has said, "*You are my Son;* today I have begotten you.'"" Kiss *the Son* or he will become angry and you will perish on the way. (Psalms 2:7, 12)

It does not mean a Son from eternity here either, but a Son born in the world, because this is a prophecy about the Lord who is going to come.

So it is called a statute about which Jehovah was making a proclamation to David. "Today" is not "from eternity" but is in time. [6] In David:

> I will place his hand on the sea. He will cry out to me, "You are my Father." I will make him the *firstborn*. (Psalms 89:25, 26, 27)

This whole psalm is about the Lord who is going to come, which is why it means the one who will call Jehovah his Father and who will be the firstborn—therefore the one who is the Son of God. [7] The same holds true elsewhere, when he is called "a shoot from the trunk of Jesse" (Isaiah 11:1), "the branch of David" (Jeremiah 23:5), "the seed of the woman" (Genesis 3:15), "the only-begotten" (John 1:18), "a priest forever" and "the Lord" (Psalms 110:4, 5).

[8] The Jewish church understood "the Son of God" to mean the Messiah whom they were awaiting, knowing that he would be born in Bethlehem. We can see from the following passages that they understood "the Son of God" to be the Messiah. In John:

> Peter said, "We believe and know that you are *the Christ, the Son of* the living *God."* (John 6:69)

In the same:

> You are *the Christ, the Son of God,* who is going to come into the world. (John 11:27)

In Matthew:

> The high priest asked Jesus whether he was *the Christ, the Son of God.* Jesus said, "I am." (Matthew 26:63, 64; Mark 14:62)

In John:

> These things have been written so that you may believe that Jesus is *the Christ, the Son of God.* (John 20:31; also Mark 1:1)

"Christ" is a Greek word and means "anointed," which is what "messiah" means in Hebrew. This is why it says in John, "We have found the Messiah (which is translated, the Christ)" (John 1:41). And in another passage, "The woman said, 'I know that *the Messiah* is coming, who is called *the Christ'*" (John 4:25).

[9] I pointed out in the first chapter [§§1–7] that the Law and the Prophets (or the whole Word of the Old Testament) are about the Lord, so the Son of God who is going to come cannot mean anything but the human nature that the Lord took upon himself in the world. [10] It follows, then,

that this is the meaning of the Son mentioned by Jehovah from heaven when Jesus was being baptized: "This is *my beloved Son,* in whom I am well pleased" (Matthew 3:17; Mark 1:11; Luke 3:22), since his human nature was being baptized. Likewise when he was transfigured: "This is *my beloved Son,* in whom I am well pleased. Hear him" (Matthew 17:5; Mark 9:7; Luke 9:35).

Then there are other passages as well, such as Matthew 8:29; 14:33; 27:43, 54; Mark 3:11; 15:39; John 1:18, 34, 49; 3:18; 5:25; 10:36; 11:4.

20 Since "the Son of God" means the Lord in the human nature that he assumed in the world, which is a divine-human nature, we can see what was meant by the Lord's frequently saying that he was sent into the world by the Father and that he had gone forth from the Father. His being sent into the world by the Father means that he was conceived by Jehovah the Father. This and nothing else is the meaning of "being sent" and "sent by the Father," as we can tell from all the places where it also says that he was doing the will of the Father and doing his works, which were overcoming the hells, glorifying his human nature, teaching the Word, and establishing a new church. The only way these things could have been done was by means of a human nature conceived by Jehovah and born of a virgin—that is, by God becoming human. Open up the passages where it says "being sent" and "sent," and you will see: Matthew 10:40, for example, and Matthew 15:24; Mark 9:37; Luke 4:43; 9:48; 10:16; John 3:17, 34; 4:34; 5:23, 24, 36, 37, 38; 6:29, 39, 40, 44, 57; 7:16, 18, 28, 29; 8:16, 18, 29, 42; 9:4; 11:41, 42; 12:44, 45, 49; 13:20; 14:24; 15:21; 16:5; 17:3, 8, 21, 23, 25; 20:21. There are also the places where the Lord calls Jehovah "Father."

21 Many people these days think of the Lord only as an ordinary person like themselves because they think only of his human nature and not at the same time of his divine nature, when in fact his human and divine natures cannot be separated. "The Lord is both God and a human being; and God and a human being in the Lord are not two but one person. He is one altogether, as the soul and the body are one human being"—this is according to what is taught throughout the Christian world, a teaching that has been ratified by councils and is called the Athanasian statement of faith. So that people will not keep thinking of the divine nature and human nature in the Lord as separate, I would ask them to read the passages from Luke cited above, and also this from Matthew:

> The birth of Jesus Christ was like this. His mother, having been betrothed to Joseph, before they came together was found to be carrying

a child from *the Holy Spirit;* and Joseph her husband, being an upright man and not wanting to disgrace her, decided to divorce her secretly. But while he was considering this, an angel of the Lord suddenly appeared to him in a dream, saying, "Joseph, son of David, do not be afraid to take Mary as your wife, because what is being born in her is from *the Holy Spirit;* and she will give birth to a son, and you will call his name 'Jesus.' He will save his people from their sins." And Joseph woke from his dream and did as the angel of the Lord had commanded, and took [Mary] as his wife. *But he did not have intercourse with her* until she had given birth to her firstborn son. And he called his name "Jesus." (Matthew 1:18–25)

We are assured by this passage and by what Luke says about the circumstances of the Lord's birth, as well as by the passages cited earlier, that the Son of God is the Jesus who was conceived by Jehovah the Father and born of the Virgin Mary, the one of whom all the Prophets and the Law prophesied until John [Matthew 11:13; Luke 16:16].

Anyone who knows what it is about the Lord that "the Son of God" means and what it is about him that "the Son of Humanity" means can see many hidden wonders in the Word, since the Lord calls himself sometimes the Son, sometimes the Son of God, and sometimes the Son of Humanity, in each case depending on the subject of the discourse.

When the subject is his divinity, or his being one with the Father, or his divine power, or faith in him, or life from him, then he calls himself "the Son" and "the Son of God," as in John 5:16–26 and elsewhere. When the subject is his suffering, though, or his judging, or his Coming, or more generally his redeeming, saving, reforming, or regenerating us, then he calls himself the Son of Humanity. This is because it then means himself as the Word.

The Lord is identified by various names in the Word of the Old Testament. There he is called Jehovah, Jah, the Lord, God, the Lord Jehovih, Jehovah Sabaoth, the God of Israel, the Holy One of Israel, the Mighty One of Jacob, Shaddai, the Rock, as well as Creator, Maker, Savior, Redeemer—always depending on the subject of the discourse. This is the case in the Word of the New Testament, too, where he is called Jesus, the Christ, the Lord, God, the Son of God, the Son of Humanity, the Prophet, and the Lamb, among other names, again always depending on the subject of the discourse.

23 So far we have been talking about why the Lord is called the Son of God. Now we must turn to why he is called the Son of Humanity.

He is called the Son of Humanity when the subject is his suffering, his judging, his Coming, or more generally his redeeming, saving, reforming, or regenerating us. This is because the Son of Humanity is the Lord as the Word; and it is as the Word that he suffered, judges, comes into the world, redeems, saves, reforms, and regenerates. What follows may serve to demonstrate that this is the case.

24 *The Lord is called the Son of Humanity when the subject is his suffering.* This we can tell from the following passages.

> Jesus said to his disciples, "Behold, we are going up to Jerusalem, and *the Son of Humanity* will be betrayed to the chief priests and to the scribes; and they will condemn him to death and hand him over to the Gentiles, and they will whip him, and spit on him, and kill him. On the third day, though, he will rise again." (Mark 10:33, 34)

Likewise elsewhere, where it foretells his suffering, as in Matthew 20:18, 19; Mark 8:31; Luke 9:22:

> Jesus said to his disciples, "Behold, the hour is at hand, and *the Son of Humanity* is being betrayed into the hands of sinners." (Matthew 26:45)

> The angel said to the women who came to the tomb, "Remember what he said to you: '*The Son of Humanity* must be betrayed into the hands of sinful people and be crucified and rise again on the third day.'" (Luke 24:6, 7)

The reason the Lord then called himself the Son of Humanity is that he allowed people to treat him the way they were treating the Word, as has already been explained more than once [§§14–16, 22–23].

25 *The Lord is called the Son of Humanity when the subject is judgment.* This we can tell from the following passages:

> When *the Son of Humanity* comes in his glory, then he will sit on the throne of his glory and set the sheep on his right and the goats on the left. (Matthew 25:31, 33)

> When *the Son of Humanity* sits on the throne of his glory, he will judge the twelve tribes of Israel. (Matthew 19:28)

> *The Son of Humanity* is going to come in the glory of his Father, and then he will repay all people according to their deeds. (Matthew 16:27)

Be wakeful at every moment, so that you may be found worthy to stand before *the Son of Humanity.* (Luke 21:36)

The Son of Humanity is coming at an hour you do not expect. (Matthew 24:44; Luke 12:40)

The Father does not judge anyone; he has given all judgment to the Son, because he is the *Son of Humanity.* (John 5:22, 27)

The reason the Lord calls himself the Son of Humanity when the subject is judgment is that all judgment is executed according to the divine truth that is in the Word. He himself says in John that this is what judges everyone:

If people hear my words but do not believe, I do not judge them. I have not come to judge the world. *The Word that I have spoken* will judge them on the last day. (John 12:47, 48)

And in another passage,

The Son of Humanity came not to condemn the world but so that the world would be saved through him. Those who believe in him are not condemned; but those who do not believe have already been condemned because they have not believed in the name of the only-begotten Son of God. (John 3:17, 18)

See *Heaven and Hell* 545–550 and 574 on the fact that the Lord never condemns anyone to hell or casts anyone into hell. Rather, evil spirits cast themselves in. The *name* of Jehovah, the Lord, or the Son of God means divine truth and therefore the Word as well, since this is from him and about him and therefore is he himself.

The Lord is called the Son of Humanity when the subject is his Coming, as we can see from the following: the disciples said to Jesus, "What will be the sign of your Coming and of the close of the age?"; and then the Lord foretold the states of the church in succession all the way to the end, saying this about its end: "Then the sign of *the Son of Humanity* will appear, and they will see *the Son of Humanity* coming in the clouds of heaven with power and glory" (Matthew 24:3, 30; Mark 13:26; Luke 21:27). The close of the age means the last time of the church; coming in the clouds of heaven with glory means opening the Word and making it clear that it was written about him alone. In Daniel:

26

I was watching, and behold, *the Son of Humanity* was coming in the clouds of the heavens! (Daniel 7:13)

In Revelation:

> Behold, he is coming with clouds, and every eye will see him. (Revelation 1:7)

This too is about *the Son of Humanity,* as we can see from verse 13 in the same chapter. Again in Revelation:

> I looked, and behold, a white cloud, and on the cloud sat someone like *the Son of Humanity.* (Revelation 14:14)

[2] In his own mind, the Lord understood "the Son of God" and "the Son of Humanity" to mean different things, as we can see from his response to the high priest:

> The high priest said to Jesus, "I put you under oath by the living God: tell us whether you are the Christ, *the Son of God.*" Jesus said to him, "It is as you said. I am. Nevertheless, I say to you, hereafter you will see *the Son of Humanity* sitting at the right hand of power and coming in the clouds of heaven." (Matthew 26:63, 64; [Mark 14:61, 62])

Here he first declares that he is the Son of God, and then says that they are going to see the Son of Humanity sitting at the right hand of power and coming in the clouds of heaven. This means that after suffering on the cross he would have access to the divine power to open the Word and establish a church, things that he could not do before because he had not yet overcome the hells and glorified his human nature.

The meaning of coming in the clouds of heaven and coming with glory has been explained in §1 of *Heaven and Hell.*

27 *The Lord is called the Son of Humanity when the subject is redemption, salvation, reformation, and regeneration,* as we can tell from the following:

> *The Son of Humanity* came to give his life as a redemption for many. (Matthew 20:28; Mark 10:45)

> *The Son of Humanity* has come to save and not to destroy. (Matthew 18:11; Luke 9:56)

> *The Son of Humanity* has come to seek and to save that which was lost. (Luke 19:10)

> *The Son of Humanity* came so that the world would be saved through him. (John 3:17)

> The one who sows good seed is *the Son of Humanity.* (Matthew 13:37)

Here the subject is redemption and salvation; and since they are effected by the Lord through the Word, he refers to himself as *the Son of Humanity*.

The Lord said that *the Son of Humanity* has power to forgive sins (Mark 2:10; Luke 5:24)—that is, power to save. He also said that he was Lord of the Sabbath because he was *the Son of Humanity* (Matthew 12:8; Mark 2:28; Luke 6:5)—because he himself is the very Word that he is then teaching.

He also says in John,

> Do not work for the food that perishes, but for the food that endures to eternal life, which *the Son of Humanity* will give you. (John 6:27)

Food means everything true and good in the teaching drawn from the Word and therefore from the Lord. This is also the meaning of the manna and of the bread that comes down from heaven, as well as the meaning of these words in the same chapter:

> Unless you eat the flesh of *the Son of Humanity* and drink his blood, you will not have life within you. (John 6:53)

The flesh or bread is good actions done from love as a result of the Word, and the blood or wine is good actions done from faith as a result of the Word, both of which come from the Lord.

[2] *"The Son of Humanity" means much the same in various other passages where it is found,* such as the following:

> Foxes have dens and birds have nests, but *the Son of Humanity* has nowhere to lay his head. (Matthew 8:20; Luke 9:58)

This means that the Word had no place among the Jews, as the Lord also says in John 8:37, and that the Word was not abiding in them, because they did not acknowledge him (John 5:38).

The Son of Humanity means the Lord as the Word in Revelation as well:

> In the midst of seven lampstands I saw one like *the Son of Humanity*, clothed with a garment down to the feet and girded about the chest with a golden band. (Revelation 1:13 and following)

In this passage various images are used to represent the Lord as the Word, so he is also called "the Son of Humanity." In David:

> Let your hand be with the man of your right hand, with *the Son of Humanity* whom you have strengthened for yourself. Then we will not turn back from you. Bring us to life. (Psalms 80:17, 18, 19)

The man of your right hand in this passage is also the Lord as the Word, and so is the Son of Humanity. He is called "the man of your right hand" because the Lord has power from divine truth, which is also the Word; and he gained divine power when he fulfilled the whole Word. That is why he also said that they would see *the Son of Humanity* sitting at the right hand of the Father with power (Mark 14:62).

28   *The reason "the Son of Humanity" means the Lord as the Word was that the prophets were also called "children of humanity."* The reason they were called this is that they represented the Lord as the Word and therefore meant the teaching of the church drawn from the Word. This is exactly how it is understood in heaven when "prophets" are mentioned in the Word. The spiritual meaning of "prophet" and also of "son of humanity" is *the teaching of the church drawn from the Word,* and when it is said of the Lord, it means *the Word itself.*

For the prophet Daniel being called a son of humanity, see Daniel 8:17.

For the prophet Ezekiel being called a son of humanity, see Ezekiel 2:1, 3, 6, 8; 3:1, 3, 4, 10, 17, 25; 4:1, 16; 5:1; 6:2; 7:2; 8:5, 6, 8, 12, 15; 11:2, 4, 15; 12:2, 3, 9, 18, 27; 13:2, 17; 14:3, 13; 15:2; 16:2; 17:2; 20:3, 4, 27, 46; 21:2, 6, 9, 12, 14, 19, 28; 22:18, 24; 23:2, 36; 24:2, 16, 25; 25:2; 26:2; 27:2; 28:2, 12, 21; 29:2, 18; 30:2, 21; 31:2; 32:2, 18; 33:2, 7, 10, 12, 24, 30; 34:2; 35:2; 36:1, 17; 37:3, 9, 11, 16; 38:2, 14; 39:1, 17; 40:4; 43:7, 10, 18; 44:5.

We can see from this that the Lord as the Divine-Human One is called "the Son of God," and as the Word is called "the Son of Humanity."

The Lord Made His Human Nature Divine out of the Divine Nature within Himself, and in This Way Became One with the Father

  ACCORDING to *the church's doctrinal statement* accepted through-out the Christian world,

> Our Lord Jesus Christ, the Son of God, is both God and a human being. Although he is God and a human being, yet he is not two, but

one Christ. He is one because the divine nature took the human nature to itself. Indeed, he is one altogether, because he is one person. Therefore as the soul and the body make one human being, so God and a human being is one Christ.

These words are quoted from the Athanasian statement of faith, which is accepted throughout the Christian world. These are that statement's essential points concerning the oneness of what is divine and what is human in the Lord. Other points concerning the Lord in that statement will be explained in their proper places [§§35, 55–61].

This shows us very clearly that according to *the statement of faith of the Christian church,* the divine and human natures in the Lord are not two but one, just as the soul and the body is one human being, and that the divine nature took the human nature to itself.

[2] It follows from this that the divine nature cannot be separated from the human or the human from the divine, because separating them would be like separating soul and body. Everyone will acknowledge this who reads the passages about the Lord's birth cited above (see §§19 and 21) from two Gospels (Luke 1:26–35 and Matthew 1:18–25). It is obvious from these passages that Jesus was conceived by Jehovah God and born of the Virgin Mary. This means that there was something divine within him, and that this was his soul.

Now, since his soul was the actual divine nature of the Father, it follows that his body or human side was made divine as well, for where the one is, the other must also be. In this way and in no other way the Father and the Son are one, the Father in the Son and the Son in the Father, and all that is the Son's is the Father's, and all that is the Father's is the Son's, as the Lord himself tells us in the Word [John 17:10].

[3] But how this union was brought about I need to explain in the following sequence:

1. The Lord from eternity is Jehovah.
2. The Lord from eternity, or Jehovah, took on a human nature for the purpose of saving us.
3. He made the human nature divine from the divine nature within himself.
4. He made the human nature divine by the trials to which he made himself vulnerable.
5. The complete union of the divine nature and the human nature in him was accomplished by the suffering on the cross, which was his last trial.

6. Step by step he took off the human nature he had taken on from his mother and put on a human nature from what was divine within him, which is the divine-human nature and the Son of God.

7. In this way, God became human on both the first [or innermost] level and the last [or outermost] level.

30   1. *The Lord from eternity is Jehovah.* This we know from the Word, since the Lord said to the Jews,

> Truly I say to you, before Abraham was, I am. (John 8:58)

And again,

> Glorify me, Father, with the glory I had with you before the world existed. (John 17:5)

This means the Lord from eternity and not the Son from eternity, because the Son is his human nature conceived by Jehovah the Father and born of the Virgin Mary in time, as explained above [§§19–20].

[2] We are assured by many passages in the Word that the Lord from eternity is Jehovah himself, a few of which passages may be cited now.

> It will be said on that day, "*This is our God;* we have waited for him to free us. [This is] *Jehovah;* we have waited for him. Let us rejoice and be glad in his salvation." (Isaiah 25:9)

We can see from this that the speakers were waiting for Jehovah God himself.

> A voice of someone in the wilderness crying out, "Prepare a pathway for *Jehovah;* make level in the desert a highway for *our God.* The glory of *Jehovah* will be revealed, and all flesh will see it together. Behold, *the Lord Jehovih* is coming in strength." (Isaiah 40:3, 5, 10; Matthew 3:3; Mark 1:3; Luke 3:4)

Here too, the Lord, who is to come, is called Jehovah.

> [3] I am Jehovah. I will make you a covenant for the people, a light for the nations. *I am Jehovah. This is my name, and I will not give my glory to another.* (Isaiah 42:6, 7, 8)

A covenant for the people and a light for the nations is the Lord in his human nature. Because this is from Jehovah and was made one with

Jehovah, it says "I am Jehovah. This is my name, and I will not give my glory to another"—that is, to no one other than himself. To give glory is to glorify, or to unite with himself.

[4] *The Lord,* whom you seek, will suddenly come to his Temple. (Malachi 3:1)

The Temple means the temple of his body, as he says in John 2:19, 21.

The Dayspring from on high has visited us. (Luke 1:78)

The Dayspring from on high is Jehovah, or the Lord from eternity.

We can see from these passages that "the Lord from eternity" means his divine nature as the source, which is called Jehovah in the Word. We will see from passages to be cited below that after his human nature had been glorified, both "the Lord" and "Jehovah" mean the divine nature and the human nature together as one, and that "the Son" by itself means the divine human nature.

2. *The Lord from eternity, or Jehovah, took on a human nature for the purpose of saving us.* There is support for this from the Word in the preceding parts of this book. It will be said elsewhere that otherwise we could not have been saved.

There are many passages in the Word that show that he took on a human nature, places where it says that he came forth from God, came down from heaven, and was sent into the world. See the following, for example:

I came forth from the Father and *have come* into the world. (John 16:28)

I proceeded forth and came from God. I have not come of myself; *he sent* me. (John 8:42)

The Father loves you because you have believed that *I came forth from God.* (John 16:27)

No one has ascended to heaven except the one who *came down from heaven.* (John 3:13)

The bread of God is the one who *comes down from heaven* and gives life to the world. (John 6:33, 35, 41, 50, 51)

The one who *comes down from above* is above all. The one who *comes down from heaven* is above all. (John 3:31)

I know the Father because *I am from him* and *he sent me.* (John 7:29)

You may see in §20 above that being sent into the world by the Father means taking on a human nature.

32 3. *The Lord made the human nature divine from the divine nature within himself.* There is support for this in many passages in the Word. Here we select passages that support the following points.

(a) *This happened step by step:*

Jesus grew and became strong in spirit and in wisdom, and the grace of God was upon him. (Luke 2:40)

Jesus increased in wisdom and age, and in favor with God and human-kind. (Luke 2:52)

[2] (b) *The divine nature worked through the human nature the way a soul works through its body:*

The Son cannot do anything on his own unless he sees the Father doing it. (John 5:19)

I do nothing of myself; as my Father taught me I say these things. The one who sent me is with me; he has not left me alone. (John 8:28, 29; 5:30)

I have not spoken on my own authority; the Father who sent me has given me a commandment regarding what I should say and what I should speak. (John 12:49, 50)

The words that I speak to you I do not speak on my own authority; the Father who dwells in me does these works. (John 14:10)

I am not alone, because the Father is with me. (John 16:32)

[3] (c) *The divine nature and the human nature worked in complete accord:*

Whatever the Father does, the Son also does in the same way. (John 5:19)

Just as the Father raises the dead and brings them to life, so also the Son brings to life those whom he wishes to. (John 5:21)

Just as the Father has life in himself, so he has also granted the Son to have life in himself. (John 5:26)

Now they know that all things you have given me are from you. (John 17:7)

[4] (d) *The divine nature was united to the human nature and the human nature to the divine:*

> "If you have known me you have also known my Father and have seen him." When Philip wanted to see the Father, Jesus said, "Have I been with you for so long, and yet you have not known me, Philip? Those who have seen me have seen the Father. Do you not believe that I am in the Father and the Father is in me? Believe me that I am in the Father and the Father is in me." (John 14:7–11)

> If I am not doing the works of my Father, do not believe me. If I am doing them, believe the works, so that you may know and believe that the Father is in me and I am in the Father. (John 10:37, 38)

> . . . so that they all may be one, as you, Father, are in me and I am in you. (John 17:21)

> On that day you will know that I am in my Father. (John 14:20)

> No one will snatch the sheep from my Father's hand. I and the Father are one. (John 10:29, 30)

> The Father loves the Son and has given all things into his hand. (John 3:35)

> All things that the Father has are mine. (John 16:15)

> All that is mine is yours, and all that is yours is mine. (John 17:10)

> You have given the Son power over all flesh. (John 17:2)

> All power has been given to me in heaven and on earth. (Matthew 28:18)

[5] (e) *We should turn to the Divine-Human One,* as we can see from the following passages:

> . . . so that all people will honor the Son just as they honor the Father. (John 5:23)

> If you had known me, you would also have known my Father. (John 8:19)

> Those who see me see the one who sent me. (John 12:45)

> If you have known me you have also known my Father, and from now on you know him and have seen him. (John 14:7)

Those who accept me accept the one who sent me. (John 13:20)

This is because no one can see the divinity itself that is called "the Father";
only the Divine-Human One can be seen. The Lord in fact said,

No one has ever seen God. The only-begotten Son, who is close to the
Father's heart, has made him visible. (John 1:18)

No one has seen the Father except the one who is with the Father. He
has seen the Father. (John 6:46)

You have never heard the Father's voice or seen what he looks like.
(John 5:37)

[6] (f) *Since the Lord made his human nature divine from the divine
nature within himself, and since we should turn to him and he is the Son of
God, we are therefore to believe in the Lord who is both Father and Son,* as
we can see from the following passages.

Jesus said that as many as accepted him, he gave them power to become
children of God and *believe in his name.* (John 1:12)

. . . so that all who *believe in him* will not perish but will have eternal
life. (John 3:15)

God loved the world so much that he gave his only-begotten Son so
that everyone who *believes in him* would have eternal life. (John 3:16)

Those who *believe in the Son* are not condemned; but those who *do not
believe* have already been condemned because *they have not believed in
the name of the only-begotten Son of God.* (John 3:18)

Those who *believe in the Son* have eternal life. Those who *do not believe
in the Son* will not see life; instead, the wrath of God abides on them.
(John 3:36)

The bread of God is the one who comes down from heaven and gives
life to the world. Those who come to me will not hunger, and those
who *believe in me* will never thirst. (John 6:33, 35)

This is the will of the one who sent me, that all those who see the Son
and *believe in him* will have eternal life, and I will raise them up on the
last day. (John 6:40)

They said to Jesus, "What should we do in order to perform the works
of God?" Jesus answered, "This is the work of God, that you *believe in
the one whom he has sent.*" (John 6:28, 29)

Truly I say to you, those who *believe in me* have eternal life. (John 6:47)

Jesus cried out, saying, "If any are thirsty, they must come to me and drink. As the Scripture has said, from the bellies of those who *believe in me* will flow rivers of living water." (John 7:37, 38)

If you do not believe that I am, you will die in your sins. (John 8:24)

Jesus said, "I am the resurrection and the life. Even if they die, those who *believe in me* will live; and anyone who lives and *believes in me* will never die." (John 11:25, 26)

Jesus said, "I have come into the world as a light so that anyone who *believes in me* will not remain in darkness." (John 12:46; 8:12)

While you have the light, *believe in the light,* so that you may become children of the light. (John 12:36)

I tell you truly, the dead will hear the voice of the Son of God, and those who hear will live. (John 5:25)

Abide in me, and I [will abide] in you. I am the vine; you are the branches. Those who abide in me and in whom I abide bear much fruit, because without me you cannot do anything. (John 15:1–5)

They were to abide in the Lord, and the Lord in them. (John 14:20; 17:23)

I am the way, the truth, and the life. No one comes to the Father except through me. (John 14:6)

[7] In these passages and all others, when it mentions "the Father" it means the divine nature that was in the Lord from his conception, which—according to the teaching embraced by the Christian world regarding faith—was like the soul within the body in human beings. The human nature that came from this divine nature is the Son of God.

Now, since this was also made divine, in order to prevent people from turning to the Father alone and thereby separating the Father from the Lord (in whom the Father dwells) in their thought, faith, and worship, the Lord went on to teach that the Father and he are one and that the Father is in him and he is in the Father, and that we are to abide in him; also that no one comes to the Father except through him. He also tells us that we are to believe in him and that we are saved by a faith focused directly on him.

[8] For many Christians, it is impossible to grasp the concept that in the Lord a human nature was made divine, primarily because they think

of "human" only in terms of the physical body and not in terms of anything spiritual. Yet all angels, who are spiritual beings, also have a completely human form, and everything divine that emanates from Jehovah
God, everything from its first [or innermost] level in heaven to its last [or
outermost] level on earth, tends to take on a human form.

On angels as human forms and on everything divine tending toward
the human form, see *Heaven and Hell* 73–77 and 453–460. There will
also be more on this subject in forthcoming works that will draw on
angelic wisdom about the Lord.

33   4. *The Lord made his human nature divine by the trials to which he
made himself vulnerable and by then constantly being victorious.* This was
discussed in §§12–14 above. I need add only the following.

Trials are battles against what is evil and false, and since what is evil
and false comes from hell, they are also battles against hell. For us too,
when we are subjected to spiritual trials, it is evil spirits from hell who are
inflicting them. We are not aware that evil spirits are behind the trials,
but an abundance of experience has taught me that they are.

[2] This is why we are rescued from hell and raised into heaven when
the Lord enables us to be victorious in our trials. This is how we become
spiritual individuals by means of our trials or battles against our evils—
how we therefore become angels.

The Lord, though, fought against all the hells with his own power
and completely tamed and subdued them; and by doing so, since at the
same time he glorified his human nature, he keeps them tamed and subdued to eternity.

[3] Before the Lord's Coming the hells had risen so far that they were
beginning to trouble even angels of heaven, and with them, everyone
who was entering the world and leaving the world. The reason for this
rise of the hells was that the church was in utter ruins, and the people of
our world were wholly devoted to evil and falsity because of their idola-
trous practices; and it is people from earth who make up hell. That is why
no one could have been saved if the Lord had not come into the world.

There is a great deal in the Psalms of David and the prophets about
these battles of the Lord, but little in the Gospels. These battles are
what we refer to as the trials that the Lord underwent, the last being
his suffering on the cross. [4] This is why the Lord is called the Savior
and Redeemer. The church is sufficiently aware of this to say that the
Lord conquered death or the Devil (that is, hell) and that he rose from
death victorious, as well as that there is no salvation apart from the

Lord. We shall see shortly that he also glorified his human nature and in this way became the Savior, Redeemer, Reformer, and Regenerator to eternity.

[5] We can see from the ample supply of passages cited in §§12–14 above that the Lord became our Savior by means of battles or trials; and there is also this from Isaiah:

> "The day of vengeance is in my heart and *the year of* my *redeemed* has arrived. I have trodden them in my wrath; I have driven their victory down into the earth." *Therefore he became their Savior.* (Isaiah 63:4, 6, 8)

This chapter is about the Lord's battles. There is also this in David:

> Lift your heads, gates! Be raised up, doors of the world, so that *the King of Glory* may come in! Who is this *King of Glory? Jehovah, strong and heroic, Jehovah, a hero in war.* (Psalms 24:7, 8)

This too is about the Lord.

5. *The complete union of the divine nature and the human nature in him was effected by the suffering on the cross, which was his last trial.*

34

Support for this proposition was provided above [§§12 14], in the chapter explaining that the Lord came into the world to subdue the hells and to glorify his human nature, and that the suffering on the cross was the last battle, by which he gained complete victory over the hells and completely glorified his human nature. Since, then, by suffering on the cross the Lord completely glorified his human nature that is, united it to the divine nature—and thereby made his human nature divine as well, it follows that he is Jehovah and God in respect to both natures. [2] That is why in so many passages in the Word Jehovah, God, or the Holy One of Israel is called the Redeemer, the Savior, or the Maker, as in the following:

> Mary said, "My soul magnifies *the Lord,* and my spirit has rejoiced in *God, my Savior.*" (Luke 1:46, 47)

> The angel said to the shepherds, "Behold, I am bringing you good news, a great joy, which will be for all people. There is born this day in the city of David a *Savior,* who is *Christ the Lord.*" (Luke 2:10, 11)

> They said, "This is truly *the Savior of the world, the Christ.*" (John 4:42)

> I, Jehovah God, am helping you; your *Redeemer* is *the Holy One of Israel.* (Isaiah 41:14)

Thus says *Jehovah,* who is *your Creator,* O Jacob, and *your Maker,* O Israel: "*I have redeemed you.* I am *Jehovah your God, the Holy One of Israel, your Savior.*" (Isaiah 43:1, 3)

Thus says Jehovah your *Redeemer, the Holy One of Israel,* "I am Jehovah, *your Holy One,* the Creator of Israel, *your King.*" (Isaiah 43:14, 15)

Thus says *Jehovah, the Holy One of Israel,* and Israel's *Maker.* (Isaiah 45:11, 15)

Thus says *Jehovah* your *Redeemer, the Holy One of Israel.* (Isaiah 48:17)

. . . so that all flesh may know that I, *Jehovah,* am your *Savior,* and *your Redeemer, the Mighty One of Jacob.* (Isaiah 49:26)

Then he will come to Zion as *the Redeemer.* (Isaiah 59:20)

. . . so that you may know that I, *Jehovah,* am *your Savior* and *your Redeemer, the Powerful One of Jacob.* (Isaiah 60:16)

Jehovah, the one who formed [me] from the womb. (Isaiah 49:5)

. . . *Jehovah,* my Rock and *my Redeemer.* (Psalms 19:14)

They remembered that God was their Rock, and *God on High their Redeemer.* (Psalms 78:35)

Thus says *Jehovah your Redeemer,* and the *one who formed* you from the womb. (Isaiah 44:24)

As for *our Redeemer, Jehovah Sabaoth* is his name, the Holy One of Israel. (Isaiah 47:4)

"With everlasting compassion I will have mercy on you," says *Jehovah, your Redeemer.* (Isaiah 54:8)

Their Redeemer is strong; Jehovah is his *name.* (Jeremiah 50:34)

Let Israel hope in *Jehovah,* because *with Jehovah* there is mercy; with him there is abundant *redemption. He will redeem* Israel from all his iniquities. (Psalms 130:7, 8)

Jehovah God is my rock, my fortress, the horn of my salvation, *my Savior.* (2 Samuel 22:2, 3)

Thus says *Jehovah, the Redeemer* of Israel, *Israel's Holy One:* "Monarchs will see and abide, because of Jehovah, who is faithful, the Holy One of Israel, who has chosen you." (Isaiah 49:7)

God is only among you, and *there is no other God.* Surely you are a hidden God, O *God of Israel, the Savior.* (Isaiah 45:14, 15)

Thus says Jehovah the King of Israel, and *Israel's Redeemer, Jehovah Sabaoth: "There is no God other than me."* (Isaiah 44:6)

I am Jehovah, and there is no Savior other than me. (Isaiah 43:11)

Am I not Jehovah? And there is no [God] other than me; and there is no Savior other than me. (Isaiah 45:21)

I am *Jehovah your God.* You are to acknowledge no God other than me; *there is no Savior other than me.* (Hosea 13:4)

Am *I* not *Jehovah?* And there is no God other than me. I am a just *God,* and *there is no Savior other than me.* Look to me so that you may *be saved,* all you ends of the earth, because *I am God and there is no other.* (Isaiah 45:21, 22)

Jehovah Sabaoth is his name, and your Redeemer, the Holy One of Israel. He will be called the God of the whole earth. (Isaiah 54:5)

[3] We can see from these passages that the Lord's divine nature called "the Father" (and here called "Jehovah" and "God") and his divine-human nature called "the Son" (and here "the Redeemer" and "the Savior" as well as "the Maker," meaning the Reformer and Regenerator) are one, not two, for it not only says "Jehovah is God" and "the Holy One of Israel is the Redeemer and Savior," it also says "Jehovah is the Redeemer and Savior." Not only that, it even calls Jehovah "the Savior" and says, "there is no Savior other than me." This clearly shows that the divine nature and the human nature in the Lord are one person and that the human nature is divine as well, since the Redeemer and Savior of the world is no other than the Lord in his divine-human nature, which is called "the Son." Redemption and salvation are properly credited to his human nature, and are called "merit and righteousness," since his human nature bore the trials and the suffering on the cross, which means that he accomplished redemption and salvation by means of his human nature.

[4] Since, then, after the union of his human nature with his inner divine nature, which was like that of soul and body in us, they were no longer two but were one person (according to the teaching of the Christian world), the Lord was Jehovah and God in both respects. This is why some passages speak of "Jehovah and the Holy One of Israel, the Redeemer

and Savior," and others say "Jehovah, the Redeemer and Savior," as you can see from the citations above.

[The Word] also speaks of *Christ, the Savior;* see Luke 2:10, 11 and John 4:42. On *God* and *the God of Israel* being *the Savior and Redeemer,* see Luke 1:47; Isaiah 45:14; 54:5; Psalms 78:35. On *Jehovah, the Holy One of Israel* being *the Savior and Redeemer,* see Isaiah 41:14; 43:3, 11, 14, 15; 48:17; 49:7; 54:5. On *Jehovah* being *the Savior, Redeemer, and Maker,* see Isaiah 44:6; 47:4; 49:26; 54:8; 63:8; Jeremiah 50:34; Psalms 19:14; 130:7, 8; 2 Samuel 22:2, 3; [Isaiah 43:1, 3; 44:24; 45:11; 49:5]. On *Jehovah God* being *the Redeemer and Savior, "and there is no Savior other than me,"* see Isaiah 43:11; 44:6; 45:14, 18, 21, 22; Hosea 13:4.

35 6. *Step by step he took off the human nature he had taken on from his mother and put on a human nature from what was divine within him, which is the divine-human nature and the Son of God.*

It is generally known that the Lord was divine and human, divine because of Jehovah the Father and human because of the Virgin Mary. That is why he was God and a human being and therefore had a divine essence and a human outward nature, the divine essence from his Father and the human nature from his mother. This meant that he was equal to the Father with respect to his divinity, but less than the Father with respect to his humanity. It also meant that, as we are taught by the so-called *Athanasian statement of faith,* this human nature from his mother was not changed into or mixed with a divine essence, since a human nature cannot be changed into or mixed with a divine essence. [2] All the same, this very statement of faith we have accepted says that the divine nature took on a human nature—that is, united itself with it as a soul with its body, so much so that they were not two but one person. It follows from this that he took off the human nature received from his mother, which was essentially like that of anyone else and therefore material, and put on a human nature from his Father, which was essentially like his divine nature and therefore substantial, thus making his human nature divine.

That is why the Lord is even called "Jehovah" and "God" in the prophetic books of the Word, and in the Word of the Gospels is called "Lord," "God," "Messiah" or "Christ," and "the Son of God," the one in whom we are to believe and by whom we are to be saved.

[3] Now, since from the beginning the Lord had a human nature from his mother and took this off step by step, while he was in this world he therefore experienced two states, one called the state of being brought low or being emptied out and one called the state of being glorified or united with the Divine called "the Father." The state of being brought

low occurred when and to the extent that he was primarily conscious of the human nature received from his mother, and the state of being glorified occurred when and to the extent that he was primarily conscious of the human nature received from his Father. In his state of being brought low he prayed to the Father as someone other than himself; while in his state of being glorified he talked with the Father as if talking with himself. In this latter state he said that the Father was in him and he in the Father and that the Father and he were one; while in his state of being brought low he bore trials, suffered on the cross, and prayed that the Father would not forsake him. This is because his divine nature could not be subject to any trial, let alone suffer on the cross.

These passages then show us that by means of his trials and the subsequent constant victories, and by means of his suffering on the cross, which was the final trial, he completely subdued the hells and completely glorified his human nature, as has been explained above.

[4] As for his taking off the human nature received from his mother and putting on the human nature received from what was divine within him called "the Father," this we can see from the fact that whenever the Lord spoke directly to his mother he did not call her "mother" but "woman." We find only three places in the Gospels where he speaks directly to his mother or about her, and in two of these he called her "woman," while in one he did not acknowledge her as his mother. As for the two in which he called her "woman," we read in John,

> Jesus' mother said to him, "They have no wine." Jesus said to her, "What have I to do with you, *woman?* My hour has not yet come." (John 2:4)

And also

> When Jesus from the cross saw his mother, and the disciple whom he loved standing by her, he said to his mother, "*Woman,* behold your son!" Then he said to the disciple, "Behold your mother!" (John 19:25, 26, 27)

The one occasion on which he did not acknowledge her is in Luke:

> They announced to Jesus, "Your mother and your brothers are standing outside and want to see you." Jesus answered and said to them, "My mother and my brothers are these who hear the Word of God and do it." (Luke 8:20, 21; Matthew 12:46–49; Mark 3:31–35)

In other passages Mary is called his mother, but never from his own mouth.

[5] There is further support for this in the fact that he did not acknowledge himself to be the son of David. In fact, we read in the Gospels,

> Jesus asked the Pharisees, saying, "What is your view of the Christ? Whose son is he?" They said to him, "David's." He said to them, "So how is it that David, in the spirit, calls him his Lord when he says, 'The Lord said to my Lord, "Sit at my right until I make your enemies a stool for your feet"'? So if David calls him 'Lord,' how is he his son?" And no one could answer him a word. (Matthew 22:41–46; Mark 12:35, 36, 37; Luke 20:41–44; Psalms 110:1)

We can see from all this that as far as his glorified human nature was concerned, the Lord was neither the son of Mary nor the son of David.

[6] He showed Peter, James, and John what his glorified human nature was like when he was transfigured before their eyes:

> His face shone like the sun and his clothing was like light. And then a voice from a cloud said, "This is my beloved Son, in whom I am well pleased. Hear him." (Matthew 17:1–8; Mark 9:2–8; Luke 9:28–36)

The Lord also looked to John "like the sun shining in its strength" (Revelation 1:16).

[7] We are assured that the Lord's human nature was glorified by what it says about his glorification in the Gospels, such as the following from John:

> The hour has come for the Son of Humanity to be glorified. He said, "Father, glorify your name." A voice came from heaven, saying, "I both have glorified it and will glorify it again." (John 12:23, 28)

It says "I both have glorified it and will glorify it again" because the Lord was glorified step by step. Again,

> After Judas went out, Jesus said, "Now the Son of Humanity is glorified, and God is glorified in him. God will also glorify him in himself and glorify him immediately." (John 13:31, 32)

Again,

> Jesus said, "Father, the hour has come. Glorify your Son, so that your Son may also glorify you." (John 17:1, 5)

And in Luke,

> Was it not necessary for Christ to suffer this and enter into his glory?
> (Luke 24:26)

These things were said about his human nature.

[8] The Lord said, "God is glorified in him" and also "God will glorify him in himself" and "Glorify your Son, so that your Son may also glorify you." The Lord said these things because the union was reciprocal, the divine nature with the human nature and the human nature with the divine. That is why he also said, "I am in the Father and the Father is in me" (John 14:10, 11) and "All that is mine is yours, and all that is yours is mine" (John 17:10); so the union was full.

It is the same with any union. Unless it is reciprocal, it is not full. This is what the union of the Lord with us and of us with the Lord must be like, as he tells us in this passage in John:

> On that day you will know that you are in me and I am in you. (John
> 14:20)

And in this passage:

> Abide in me, and I [will abide] in you. Those who abide in me and in
> whom I abide bear much fruit. (John 15:4, 5)

[9] Because the Lord's human nature was glorified—that is, made divine—on the third day after his death he rose again with his whole body, which is not true of any human being, since we rise again with our spirit only and not with our body.

So that we should know this, and so that no one should doubt that the Lord rose again with his whole body, he not only said so through the angels who were in the tomb but also showed himself to the disciples in his human form with his body, saying to them when they thought they were seeing a spirit,

> "See my hands and my feet—that it is I myself. Touch me and see,
> because a spirit does not have flesh and bones as you see I have." And
> when he had said this, he showed them his hands and his feet. (Luke
> 24:39, 40; John 20:20)

And again,

> Jesus said to Thomas, "Reach your finger here, and look at my hands;
> and reach out your hand and put it into my side; and do not be

unbelieving, but believing." Then Thomas said, "My Lord and my God." (John 20:27, 28)

[10] To make it even clearer that he was not a spirit but a person, he said to the disciples,

> "Have you any food here?" They gave him a piece of broiled fish and some honeycomb, and he took it and ate in their presence. (Luke 24:41, 42, 43)

Since his body was no longer material but had become divine substance, he came to the disciples when the doors were closed (John 20:19, 26) and disappeared after they had seen him (Luke 24:31).

Once the Lord was in this state, he was carried up and sat down at the right hand of God, for it says in Luke,

> It happened that, while Jesus blessed his disciples, he was parted from them and carried up into heaven. (Luke 24:51)

and in Mark,

> After he had spoken to them, he was carried up into heaven and sat down at the right hand of God. (Mark 16:19)

Sitting down at the right hand of God means gaining divine omnipotence.

[11] Since the Lord rose into heaven with his divine and human natures united into one and sat at the right hand of God (which means gaining omnipotence), it follows that his human substance or essence is now just like his divine substance or essence.

To think otherwise would be like thinking that his divine nature was raised into heaven and sits at the right hand of God, but not together with his human nature. This is contrary to Scripture and also contrary to the Christian teaching that in Christ God and a human being are like the soul and the body. To separate them is also contrary to sound reason.

It is this union of the Father with the Son, or of the divine nature with the human nature, that is meant in the following passages:

> I came forth from the Father and have come into the world. Again, I leave the world and go to the Father. (John 16:28)

> I go (or come) to the one who sent me. (John 7:33; 16:5, 16; 17:11, 13; 20:17)

What then if you were to see the Son of Humanity ascend where he was before? (John 6:62)

No one has ascended to heaven except the one who came down from heaven. (John 3:13)

Every one of us who is saved ascends to heaven, though not on our own, but rather through the Lord's power. Only the Lord ascended on his own.

7. *In this way, God became human on both the first [or innermost] level* **36** *and the last [or outermost] level.*

It is explained at some length in *Heaven and Hell* [§§78–86] that God is human and that because of God all angels and spirits are human, and there will be more on this topic in the books about angelic wisdom.

While from the beginning God was human on the first [or innermost] level, he was not yet human on the last [or outermost] level. After he took on a human nature in the world, though, he also became human on the last [or outermost] level. This follows from what has been shown above [§§29–35], namely, that the Lord united his human nature with his divine nature and in this way made his human nature divine as well. [2] That is why the Lord is called the Beginning and the End, the First and the Last, and the Alpha and the Omega. This is in the Book of Revelation:

"I am the Alpha and the Omega, the Beginning and the End," says the Lord, "who is and who was and who is to come, the Almighty." (Revelation 1:8, 11)

When John saw the Son of Humanity in the midst of the seven lampstands,

[John] fell at his feet as dead, but [the Son of Humanity] laid his right hand on him, saying, "I am the First and the Last." (Revelation 1:13, 17; 2:8; 21:6)

Behold, I am coming quickly, to give to all according to what they have done. I am the Alpha and the Omega, the Beginning and the End, the First and the Last. (Revelation 22:12, 13)

And in Isaiah,

Thus says Jehovah the King of Israel, and Israel's Redeemer, Jehovah Sabaoth: "I am the First and the Last." (Isaiah 44:6; 48:12)

The Lord Is God Himself,
the Source and Subject of the Word

37 IN the first chapter [§§1–7] I undertook to show that the whole of Sacred Scripture is about the Lord and that the Lord is the Word. At this point I need to set this forth further with passages from the Word where the Lord is called Jehovah, the God of Israel and Jacob, the Holy One of Israel, Lord, and God, as well as King, Jehovah's Anointed, and David.

By way of preface I may observe that I have been granted the opportunity to read through all the prophets and the Psalms, to reflect on the individual verses and see what they were about; and it became clear that they were about nothing but the church that had been established and was to be established by the Lord, about the Lord's Coming, his battles, glorification, redemption, and salvation and about the heaven that comes from him, together with their opposites. Since these are all works of the Lord, I could see that the whole of Sacred Scripture is about the Lord and that therefore the Lord is the Word.

[2] The only people who can see this, though, are the ones who enjoy enlightenment from the Lord and who are also acquainted with the Word's spiritual meaning. All the angels in heaven are aware of this meaning, so when one of us is reading the Word, that and that alone is what they grasp. There are always angels and spirits with us, and since they are spiritual beings, they understand spiritually what we understand in earthly terms.

From the passages cited earlier, in the first chapter (§§1–7), we can see only dimly, as though through a screen, that the whole of Sacred Scripture is about the Lord. The passages about the Lord now to be cited show that he is often called "Lord" and "God." It may be very clear from this that he is the one who spoke through the prophets, in whose books it says again and again, "Jehovah spoke," "Jehovah said," and "the saying of Jehovah."

[3] We can see *that the Lord existed before his coming into the world* from the following passages:

John the Baptist said of the Lord, "This is the one who is to come after me, who was before me; I am not worthy to undo the strap of his sandal." And "This is the one of whom I said, 'One is coming after me, who was before me and was greater than me.'" (John 1:27, 30)

In the Book of Revelation:

[The elders] fell down before the throne on which the Lord was, saying, "We give you thanks, O Lord God Almighty, who is and who was and who is to come." (Revelation 11:16, 17)

In Micah:

As for you, Bethlehem Ephrata, as little as you are among the thousands of Judah, one will come forth from you for me who will become the ruler in Israel; his coming forth is from ancient times, from the days of eternity. (Micah 5:2)

We can also see from the Lord's words in the Gospels that he existed before Abraham [John 8:58], that he had glory with the Father before the foundation of the world [John 17.5, 24], that he came forth from the Father [John 16:28], that the Word was with God from the beginning and that the Word was God [John 1:1], and that the Word became flesh [John 1:14]. The passages that follow will serve to show that the Lord is called Jehovah, the God of Israel and of Jacob, the Holy One of Israel, God, and the Lord, as well as King, Jehovah's Anointed, and David.

We can see from the following passages that the Lord is called "Jehovah": **38**

Thus says *Jehovah*, who is your Creator, O Jacob, and your Maker, O Israel: "*I have redeemed* you. I am *Jehovah* your God, the Holy One of Israel, your *Savior*." (Isaiah 43:1, 3)

I am *Jehovah*, your Holy One, *the Creator of Israel*, [your King. (Isaiah 43:15)]

[Thus says *Jehovah*, the Holy One of Israel,] and Israel's *Maker*, [the *Savior*] . . . (Isaiah 45:11, 15)

. . . so that all flesh may know that I, *Jehovah*, am your *Savior*, and your *Redeemer*, the Mighty One of Jacob. (Isaiah 49:26)

. . . so that you may know that I, *Jehovah*, am your *Savior* and your *Redeemer*, the Powerful One of Jacob. (Isaiah 60:16)

. . . *Jehovah, the one who formed [me]* from the womb. (Isaiah 49:5)

. . . *Jehovah*, my rock and my *Redeemer*. (Psalms 19:14)

Thus says *Jehovah* your Maker and the *one who formed* you from the womb. Thus says *Jehovah,* the King of Israel, and Israel's *Redeemer, Jehovah Sabaoth.* (Isaiah 44:2, 6)

As for our *Redeemer, Jehovah Sabaoth is his name,* the Holy One of Israel. (Isaiah 47:4)

"With everlasting compassion I will have mercy [on you]," says Jehovah, your *Redeemer.* (Isaiah 54:8)

Their Redeemer is strong; Jehovah is his name. (Jeremiah 50:34)

Jehovah God is my rock, my fortress, the horn of my salvation, my *Savior.* (2 Samuel 22:2, 3)

Thus says *Jehovah* your *Redeemer, the Holy One of Israel.* (Isaiah 43:14; 48:17)

Thus says *Jehovah, the Redeemer* of Israel, Israel's Holy One: "Monarchs will see . . ." (Isaiah 49:7)

I am *Jehovah,* and there is no *Savior* other than me. (Isaiah 43:11)

Am I not *Jehovah?* And there is no [God] other than me; and there is no *Savior* other than me. Look to me so that you may *be saved,* all you ends of the earth. (Isaiah 45:21, 22)

I am *Jehovah* your God; there is no *Savior* other than me. (Hosea 13:4)

You have redeemed me, O *Jehovah* of truth. (Psalms 31:5)

Let Israel hope in *Jehovah,* for with *Jehovah* there is mercy; with him there is abundant *redemption. He will redeem* Israel from all his iniquities. (Psalms 130:7, 8)

Jehovah Sabaoth is his name, and your *Redeemer,* the Holy One of Israel. He will be called the God of the whole earth. (Isaiah 54:5)

In these passages, Jehovah is called Redeemer and Savior; and since the Lord alone is Redeemer and Savior, it is he who is meant by "Jehovah."

We can also see that the Lord is Jehovah—that is, that Jehovah is the Lord—from the following passages.

A shoot [will go forth] from the trunk of Jesse, and a sprout from its roots will bear fruit. *The spirit of Jehovah* will rest upon him. (Isaiah 11:1, 2)

It will be said on that day, "Behold, this is our God; we have waited for him to set us free. [This is] *Jehovah; we have waited for him. Let us rejoice and be glad in his salvation."* (Isaiah 25:9)

A voice of someone in the wilderness crying out, "Prepare a pathway for *Jehovah;* make level in the desert a highway for our God." *The glory of Jehovah* will be revealed, and all flesh will see it. Behold, *the Lord Jehovih* is coming in strength, and his arm will rule for him. (Isaiah 40:3, 5, 10)

I am *Jehovah.* I will make you a covenant for the people, a light for the nations. I am *Jehovah.* This is my name, and *I will not give my glory to another.* (Isaiah 42:6, 7, 8)

Behold, the days [are coming] when I will raise up for David a righteous branch who will rule as king, and prosper, and bring about judgment and justice on earth. And this is his name: they will call him *"Jehovah our Righteousness."* (Jeremiah 23:5, 6; 33:15, 16)

As for you, Bethlehem Ephrata, one will come forth from you for me who will become the ruler in Israel. He will stand firm and feed [his flock] in *the strength of Jehovah.* (Micah 5:2, 4)

A Child has been born to us; a Son has been given to us. Leadership is upon his shoulder; and his name will be called God, Hero, *Father of Eternity,* on the throne of David, to establish and found it in judgment and in justice, from now on, even to eternity. (Isaiah 9:6, 7)

Jehovah will go forth and fight against the nations, and his feet will stand on the Mount of Olives, which faces Jerusalem. (Zechariah 14:3, 4)

Lift your heads, gates, and be raised up, doors of the world, so that the King of Glory may come in! Who is this King of Glory? *Jehovah,* strong and heroic, *Jehovah,* a hero in war. (Psalms 24:7–10)

On that day *Jehovah Sabaoth* will become an ornate crown and a beautiful diadem for the remnant of his people. (Isaiah 28:5)

I will send you Elijah the prophet before the great *day of Jehovah* comes. (Malachi 4:5)

There are other passages as well where it says that *the day of Jehovah* is great and near, like Ezekiel 30:3; Joel 2:11; Amos 5:18, 20; and Zephaniah 1:7, 14, 15, 18.

39   *We can see that the Lord is called "the God of Israel" and "the God of Jacob" from the following passages:*

Moses took the blood and sprinkled it on the people and said, "This is the blood of the covenant that Jehovah has made with you." And they saw *the God of Israel,* under whose feet there was something like a work of sapphire stone and like the substance of heaven. (Exodus 24:8, 9, 10)

The crowds were amazed when they saw the mute speaking, the lame walking, and the blind seeing; and they glorified *the God of Israel.* (Matthew 15:31)

Blessed is *the Lord God of Israel,* because he has visited and freed his people Israel, when he raised up the horn of our salvation in the house of David. (Luke 1:68, 69)

I will give you treasures of darkness and the hidden wealth of secret places so that you may recognize that I, Jehovah, who have called you by your name, am *the God of Israel.* (Isaiah 45:3)

. . . the house of Jacob, people who swear by the name of Jehovah and of the God of Israel, for they are called by the name of the holy city and rely on *the God of Israel:* Jehovah Sabaoth is his name. (Isaiah 48:1, 2)

Jacob will see his descendants in his midst. They will sanctify my name and will sanctify the Holy One of Jacob; and they will fear *the God of Israel.* (Isaiah 29:23)

In the very last of days many people will come and say, "Come, and let us go up to the mountain of Jehovah, to the house of *the God of Jacob,* who will teach us about his ways so that we may walk in his paths." (Isaiah 2:3; Micah 4:2)

. . . so that all flesh may know that I, Jehovah, am your Savior, and your *Redeemer, the Mighty One of Jacob.* (Isaiah 49:26)

I, Jehovah, am your Savior and your Redeemer, the *Powerful One of Jacob.* (Isaiah 60:16)

In the presence of the Lord you give birth, O earth, in the presence of *the God of Jacob.* (Psalms 114:7)

David swore to Jehovah and made a vow to *the Mighty One of Jacob,* "[God forbid] that I enter the tent of my home until I have found a place for Jehovah, a dwelling for the *Mighty One of Jacob.*" We have heard of him in Ephrata [that is, Bethlehem]. (Psalms 132:2, 3, 5, 6)

Blessed be *the God of Israel;* the whole earth will be full of his glory. (Psalms 72:18, 19)

There are also many other passages where the Lord is called "God of Israel," "Redeemer," and "Savior," such as Luke 1:47; Isaiah 45:15; 54:5; Psalms 78:35; and many other places where we find only "the God of Israel," as in Isaiah 17:6; 21:10, 17; 24:15; 29:23; Jeremiah 7:3; 9:15; 11:3; 13:12; 16:9; 19:3, 15; 23:2; 24:5; 25:15, 27; 29:4, 8, 21, 25; 30:2; 31:23; 32:14, 15, 36; 33:4; 34:2, 13; 35:13, 17, 18, 19; 37:7; 38:17; 39:16; 42:9, 15, 18; 43:10; 44:2, 7, 11, 25; 48:1; 50:18; 51:33; Ezekiel 8:4; 9:3; 10:19, 20; 11:22; 43:2; 44:2; Zephaniah 2:9; Psalms 41:13; 59:5; 68:8.

We can see that the Lord is called the Holy One of Israel from the following passages. **40**

The angel said to Mary, "The *Holy One* that is born from you will be called the Son of God." (Luke 1:35)

I saw in visions, and behold, a Watcher, a *Holy One,* coming down from heaven. (Daniel 4:13, 23)

God will come from Teman and the *Holy One* from Mount Paran. (Habakkuk 3:3)

I am Jehovah, your *Holy One,* the Creator of Israel, [your King]. (Isaiah 43:15)

[Thus says Jehovah, *the Holy One of Israel,*] and Israel's Maker, [the Savior]. (Isaiah 45:11, 15)

Thus says Jehovah, the Redeemer of Israel, Israel's *Holy One.* (Isaiah 49:7)

I am Jehovah your God, the *Holy One of Israel,* your Savior. (Isaiah 43:1, 3)

As for our Redeemer, Jehovah Sabaoth is his name, the *Holy One of Israel.* (Isaiah 47:4)

Thus says Jehovah your Redeemer, the *Holy One of Israel.* (Isaiah 43:14; 48:17)

Jehovah Sabaoth is his name, and your Redeemer, the *Holy One of Israel.* (Isaiah 54:5)

They tested God and the *Holy One of Israel.* (Psalms 78:41)

They have abandoned Jehovah and have angered the *Holy One of Israel.* (Isaiah 1:4)

They said, "Make the *Holy One of Israel* cease from our presence." Therefore thus said the *Holy One of Israel* . . . (Isaiah 30:11, 12)

. . . those who say, "Let him hasten his work so that we may see; let the counsel of the *Holy One of Israel* draw near and arrive." (Isaiah 5:19)

On that day they will rely on Jehovah, the *Holy One of Israel,* in truth. (Isaiah 10:20)

Shout and rejoice, daughter of Zion, because the *Holy One of Israel* is great in your midst. (Isaiah 12:6)

The God of Israel has said, "On that day people will look back to their Maker, and their eyes will look toward the *Holy One of Israel.*" (Isaiah 17:7)

The meek will increase their joy in Jehovah, and the poor of the people will rejoice in the *Holy One of Israel.* (Isaiah 29:19; 41:16)

Nations will run to you because of Jehovah your God and because of the *Holy One of Israel.* (Isaiah 55:5)

The islands will trust in me to bring your children from afar for the name of Jehovah Sabaoth and the *Holy One of Israel.* (Isaiah 60:9)

Their land is full of sin against the *Holy One of Israel.* (Jeremiah 51:5)

There are many other instances elsewhere.

The Holy One of Israel means the Lord in his divine-human nature, since the angel Gabriel said to Mary, "The *Holy One* that is born from you will be called the Son of God" (Luke 1:35). As for Jehovah and the Holy One of Israel being one and the same even though they are given different names, this is quite clear from the passages just cited where it says that Jehovah is the Holy One of Israel.

41 We can see *that the Lord is called Lord and God* from many passages, so many that to cite them all would fill pages. These few may suffice. In John:

When Thomas at the Lord's bidding looked at his hands and touched his side, he said, "*My Lord and my God.*" (John 20:27, 28)

In David,

> They remembered that *God* was their Rock, and *God on High* their *Redeemer.* (Psalms 78:35)

And in Isaiah,

> Jehovah Sabaoth is his name, and your *Redeemer,* the Holy One of Israel. *He will be called the God of the whole earth.* (Isaiah 54:5)

We can see this also from the fact that they worshiped him and fell on their faces before him—Matthew 9:18; 14:33; 15:25; 28:9; Mark 1:40; 5:22; 7:25; 10:17; Luke 17:15, 16; John 9:38. And in David,

> We heard of him in Ephrata; let us enter his dwelling and *bow down at the stool for his feet.* (Psalms 132:6, 7)

It is much the same in heaven, as described in the Book of Revelation:

> I was in the spirit; and behold, a throne set in heaven, and one sat on the throne. He was like a jasper and a sardius stone, and there was a rainbow around the throne, in appearance like an emerald. And the twenty-four elders *fell down* before the one who sits on the throne and *worshiped the one who lives forever and ever, and cast their crowns before the throne.* (Revelation 4:2, 3, 10)

And again,

> I saw in the right hand of the one who sat on the throne a scroll, written inside and on the back, sealed with seven seals. And no one was able to open the scroll. Then one of the elders said, "Behold, the Lion of the tribe of Judah, the Root of David, has prevailed to open the scroll and to loose its seven seals." And I saw in the midst of the throne a Lamb standing. He came and took the scroll, and *[the twenty-four elders] fell down before the Lamb and worshiped the one who lives forever and ever.* (Revelation 5:1, 3, 5, 6, 7, 8, 14)

The reason *the Lord is called King and [Jehovah's] Anointed* is that he **42** was the Messiah or Christ, and "Messiah" or "Christ" means "King" and "Anointed One." That is also why "King" in the Word means the Lord. *Much the same was meant by David,* who was king over Judah and over Israel.

We can see from many passages in the Word that the Lord was called "King" and "Jehovah's Anointed." That is why it says in Revelation, "The Lamb will overcome them, because he is *Lord of Lords and King of Kings*" (Revelation 17:14); and again, the one who sat on the white horse "had on his robe a name written—*King of Kings and Lord of Lords*" (Revelation 19:16).

It is because the Lord is called "King" that heaven and the church are called *his kingdom* and his coming into the world is called *the gospel of the kingdom.*

On heaven and the church being called his kingdom, see Matthew 12:28; 16:28; Mark 1:14, 15; 9:1; 15:43; Luke 1:33; 4:43; 8:1, 10; 9:2, 11, 60; 10:11; 16:16; 19:11; 21:31; 22:18; 23:51; and in Daniel:

> God will raise up a *kingdom* that will never be destroyed. It will crush and devour all these other kingdoms, and it will stand forever. (Daniel 2:44)

In the same,

> I was watching in the night visions, and behold, someone like the Son of Humanity was coming with the clouds of the heavens. To him was given *dominion* and glory and a *kingdom,* so that all peoples, nations, and tongues would worship him. His *dominion* is an everlasting *dominion,* and his *kingdom* is one that will not perish. (Daniel 7:13, 14, 27)

On his Coming being called "the gospel of the kingdom," see Matthew 4:23; 9:35; 24:14.

43 *We can see from the following passages that the Lord is called "David."*

> On that day they will serve Jehovah their God and David their king, whom I will raise up for them. (Jeremiah 30:9)

> Then the children of Israel will turn back and seek Jehovah their God and David their king; with fear they will come to Jehovah and his goodness at the very last of days. (Hosea 3:5)

> I will raise up one shepherd over them, who will feed them: my servant David. He will feed them and be their shepherd. I, Jehovah, will be their God, and David will be the leader in their midst. (Ezekiel 34:23, 24)

> So that they become my people, and I become their God, my servant David will be king over them; there will be one shepherd for them all. Then they will dwell in the land, they and their children and their children's children forever, and David will be their leader forever. And

I will make a covenant of peace with them, and it will be an everlasting covenant with them. (Ezekiel 37:23–26)

I will make an everlasting covenant with you, the sure mercies of David. Behold, I have made him a witness to the peoples, a prince and a lawmaker to the nations. (Isaiah 55:3, 4)

On that day I will raise up the fallen tent of David and patch its holes; I will restore its ruins and build it as it was in ancient days. (Amos 9:11)

The house of David will be like God, like the angel of Jehovah before them. (Zechariah 12:8)

On that day a fountain will be opened for the house of David. (Zechariah 13:1)

Once people realize that "David" means the Lord, they can know why David so often wrote about the Lord in his psalms when he was writing about himself. See Psalm 89, for example, where we find,

I have made a covenant with my chosen one, I have sworn to David my servant, "I will establish your seed even to eternity and build your throne for generation after generation. And the heavens will bear witness to your wondrous work, and to [your] truth, in the congregation of the saints." Then you spoke to your holy one in a vision and said, "I have put [ability to] help in a mighty one; I have raised up a chosen one from among the people. I have found David, my servant; I have anointed him with my holy oil. With him my hand will be strong; my arm will strengthen him also. My truth and my mercy will be with him, and his horn will be exalted in my name. And I will place his hand on the sea and his right hand on the rivers. He will cry out to me, 'You are my Father, my God, and the Rock of my salvation.' I will also make him the firstborn, high above the monarchs of the earth. My covenant will be established with him. I will make his seed endure to eternity and his throne as the days of the heavens. I have sworn once by my holiness; I will not lie to David. His seed will endure forever and his throne will be like the sun before me; it will be as established as the moon to eternity and a faithful witness in the clouds." (Psalms 89:3, 4, 5, 19, 20, 21, 24, 25, 26, 27, 28, 29, 35, 36, 37)

There is similar material in other psalms, such as Psalm 45:2–17, Psalm 122:4, 5, and Psalm 132:8–18.

God Is One, and the Lord Is God

45 ON the basis of the quite ample number of passages from the Word presented in the preceding chapter [§§37–44], we can determine that the Lord is called Jehovah, the God of Israel and of Jacob, the Holy One of Israel, Lord and God, as well as King, [Jehovah's] Anointed, and David, all of which enables us to see (though as yet through a kind of veil) that the Lord is God himself, the source and subject of the Word.

All the same, it is generally acknowledged everywhere in the whole world that God is one, and no one of sound reason denies this. What now remains to be done, then, is to support this from the Word and further, to show that the Lord is God.

[2] 1. *The following passages from the Word show that God is one.*

Jesus said, "The first of all the commandments is 'Hear, O Israel, *the Lord our God, the Lord is one;* therefore you are to love the Lord your God with all your heart and with all your soul.'" (Mark 12:29, 30)

Hear, O Israel, *Jehovah our God is one Jehovah;* you are to love Jehovah your God with all your heart and with all your soul. (Deuteronomy 6:4, 5)

Someone came to Jesus and said, "Good Teacher, what good thing should I do in order to have eternal life?" Jesus said to him, "Why do you call me good? *No one is good except the one God."* (Matthew 19:16, 17)

. . . so that all the kingdoms of the earth may acknowledge that *you alone are Jehovah.* (Isaiah 37:20)

I am Jehovah and there is no other. There is no God other than me. [I have prepared you] so that people will know from the rising of the sun to its setting that there is no God other than me. I am Jehovah and there is no other. (Isaiah 45:5, 6)

Jehovah Sabaoth, God of Israel, dwelling between the angel guardians, *you alone are God* over all the kingdoms of the earth. (Isaiah 37:16)

Is there any God other than me? Or any other Rock? I do not know of one. (Isaiah 44:8)

Who is God, except Jehovah? Who is the Rock, if it is not our God? (Psalms 18:31)

[3] 2. *The following passages from the Word show that the Lord is God.*

God is only among you, *and there is no God except him.* Surely you are a hidden God, O God of Israel, *the Savior.* (Isaiah 45:14, 15)

Am I not Jehovah? And *there is no God other than me.* I am a just God, and *there is no Savior other than me.* Look to me so that you may *be saved,* all you ends of the earth, because *I am God and there is no other.* (Isaiah 45:21, 22)

I am Jehovah, and *there is no Savior other than me.* (Isaiah 43:11)

I am Jehovah your God. You are to acknowledge no God other than me; *there is no Savior other than me.* (Hosea 13:4)

Thus says Jehovah the King of Israel, and Israel's *Redeemer,* Jehovah Sabaoth: "I am the First and the Last, and *there is no God other than me."* (Isaiah 44:6)

Jehovah Sabaoth is his name, and the *Redeemer,* the Holy One of Israel. He will be called the God of the whole earth. (Isaiah 54:5)

On that day Jehovah will become king over all the earth. On that day Jehovah will be one, and his name one. (Zechariah 14:9)

Since the Lord alone is Savior and Redeemer, and since it says that Jehovah and no one else is that one, it follows that the one God is no other than the Lord.

The Holy Spirit Is the Divine Nature That Emanates from the Lord and Is the Lord Himself

JESUS said in Matthew,

46

All power has been given to me in heaven and on earth. Go forth, therefore, and make disciples of all the nations, baptizing them in the name of the Father, the Son, and the Holy Spirit, teaching them to observe all things that I have commanded you; and behold, I am with you all the days, even to the close of the age. (Matthew 28:18, 19, 20)

Up to this point I have shown that the divine nature called the Father and the divine nature called the Son are one in the Lord. I therefore need now to show that the Holy Spirit is the same as the Lord.

[2] The reason the Lord said that they were to baptize in the name of the Father, the Son, and the Holy Spirit is that there is a threeness or trinity in the Lord. There is the divine nature that is called the Father, the divine-human nature that is called the Son, and the emanating divine nature that is called the Holy Spirit. The divine nature that is the Father and the divine nature that is the Son is the divine nature as the source, while the emanating divine nature that is the Holy Spirit is the divine nature as means.

In the booklets *Divine Providence* and *Omnipotence, Omnipresence, and Omniscience,* you will see more on the point that the only divine nature that emanates from the Lord is the divine nature that is he himself—it is a matter that takes more than a few words to explain.

[3] We can illustrate this threeness in the Lord by comparison with angels. They have souls and bodies and also emanations that radiate from them, emanations that are their own selves extending beyond themselves. I have been granted an abundance of knowledge about this emanation, but this is not the place to present it.

[4] After death, everyone who turns to God is first taught by angels that the Holy Spirit is none other than the Lord and that "going forth" and "emanating" is nothing but enlightening and teaching by means of presence, a presence that depends on our acceptance of the Lord. So after death, many people leave behind the concept of the Holy Spirit that they had formed in the world and accept the idea that it is the Lord's presence with us through angels and spirits, a presence from and by means of which people are enlightened and taught.

[5] Then too, it is common practice in the Word to name two divine beings, sometimes three, who are nevertheless one, such as Jehovah and God, Jehovah and the Holy One of Israel, Jehovah and the Mighty One of Jacob, as well as God and the Lamb; and because they are one it says elsewhere that Jehovah alone is God, Jehovah alone is the Holy One and is the Holy One of Israel, and there is no God other than him. Sometimes God is called the Lamb and sometimes the Lamb is called God, the latter in the Book of Revelation and the former in the prophets.

[6] We can see that it is the Lord alone who is meant by "the Father, the Son, and the Holy Spirit" in Matthew 28:19 from what precedes and follows that verse. In the preceding verse the Lord says, "All power has been given to me in heaven and on earth," and in the next verse the Lord

says, "Behold, I am with you all the days, even to the close of the age."
So he is talking about himself alone, saying this so that they would know
that the trinity was in him.

[7] To make it known that the Holy Spirit is no divine thing other
than the Lord himself, I need to show what "spirit" means in the Word.

1. "Spirit," in a broad sense, refers to an individual's life.
2. Since our life varies depending on our state, "spirit" means the variable attitude we take toward life.
3. It also means the life of those who have been regenerated, which is called spiritual life.
4. Where "spirit" is used in speaking of the Lord, though, it means his divine life and therefore the Lord himself.
5. Specifically, it means the life of his wisdom, which is called divine truth.
6. Jehovah himself—that is, the Lord—spoke the Word through prophets.

1. *"Spirit" refers to an individual's life.* This is clear from the fact that
we commonly speak of "yielding up the spirit" when someone dies. In
this sense, then, "spirit" means the life of our breathing. In fact, the word
"spirit" is derived from [a word for] breathing, which is why in Hebrew
the word that means "spirit" also means "wind."

We have two inner springs of life. One is the motion of the heart,
and the other is the breathing of the lungs. The life that depends on the
breathing of the lungs is the one properly meant by "spirit" and also by
"soul." In the appropriate place there will be a description of the way this
is coordinated with our cognitive thinking, while the life dependent on the
motion of the heart is coordinated with the love associated with our will.

[2] It is clear from the following passages that "spirit" in the Word
refers to an individual's life.

> You gather in their *spirit;* they breathe their last and return to dust. (Psalms 104:29)

> He remembered that they were flesh, a *spirit* that departs and does not return. (Psalms 78:39)

> When their *spirit* leaves, they will return to the earth. (Psalms 146:4)

> Hezekiah expressed grief that *"the life of his spirit"* was departing. (Isaiah 38:16)

47

The spirit of Jacob came back to life. (Genesis 45:27)

A molded image is a lie, and there is no *spirit* within it. (Jeremiah 51:17)

The Lord Jehovih said to the dry bones, "I will put *spirit* into you so that you will live. Come from the four winds, *O spirit, and breathe on these people who have been killed,* and they will live"; and *the spirit* came into them, and they came back to life. (Ezekiel 37:5, 6, 9, 10)

When Jesus took the daughter's hand, her *spirit* returned, and she arose immediately. (Luke 8:54, 55)

48   2. *Since our life varies depending on our state, "spirit" means the variable attitude we take toward life.* For example:
(a) *Living wisely.*

Bezalel was filled with *the spirit of wisdom,* intelligence, and knowledge. (Exodus 31:3)

You shall speak to all who are wise at heart, everyone whom I have filled with *the spirit of wisdom.* (Exodus 28:3)

Joshua was filled with *the spirit of wisdom.* (Deuteronomy 34:9)

Nebuchadnezzar said of Daniel that [*the spirit of the holy gods* was in him]. (Daniel 4:8)

[Belshazzar's queen said of Daniel that] there was an *excellent spirit* of knowledge, intelligence, and *wisdom* in him. (Daniel 5:11–12, 14)

Those who go astray *in spirit* will know intelligence. (Isaiah 29:24)

[2] (b) *Living [under the influence of some particular] inspiration.*

Jehovah *has stirred up the spirit* of the kings of Media. (Jeremiah 51:11)

Jehovah *stirred up the spirit* of Zerubbabel and the *spirit* of all the remnant of the people. (Haggai 1:14)

I am putting the spirit into the king of Assyria [to cause him] to hear a rumor and return to his own land. (Isaiah 37:7)

Jehovah *hardened the spirit* of King Sihon. (Deuteronomy 2:30)

What *is rising up in* your *spirit* will never happen. (Ezekiel 20:32)

[3] (c) *Living in a state of freedom.*

The four beasts seen by the prophet, which were angel guardians, went wherever *the spirit* wanted to go. (Ezekiel 1:12, 20)

[4] (d) *Living in fear, sorrow, or anger.*

. . . so that every heart will melt, all hands will slacken, and *every spirit will recoil.* (Ezekiel 21:7)

My *spirit has fainted* within me; my heart is stupefied inside me. (Psalms 142:3; 143:4)

My *spirit is wasting away.* (Psalms 143:7)

I, Daniel, *was grieved in* my *spirit.* (Daniel 7:15)

The spirit of Pharaoh was disturbed. (Genesis 41:8)

Nebuchadnezzar said, "*My spirit is troubled.*" (Daniel 2:3)

I went in bitterness, *in the heat of* my *spirit.* (Ezekiel 3:14)

[5] (e) *Living in subjection to various evil mental states.*

. . . who has *no guile in his spirit.* (Psalms 32:2)

Jehovah has mixed together in their midst *a spirit of perversities.* (Isaiah 19:14)

[The Lord Jehovih] says, "[Woe] to the *foolish* prophets, who follow their own *spirit.*" (Ezekiel 13:3)

The prophet is foolish; *the man of the spirit is insane.* (Hosea 9:7)

Keep watch over *your spirit,* and do not act treacherously. (Malachi 2:16)

A spirit of whoredom has led them astray. (Hosea 4:12)

There is *a spirit of whoredom* in their midst. (Hosea 5:4)

When a *spirit of jealousy* has come over him . . . (Numbers 5:14)

A man who is a wanderer *in spirit* and speaks lies . . . (Micah 2:11)

. . . a generation whose *spirit was not constant with God* . . . (Psalms 78:8)

He has poured *a spirit of sleepiness* over them. (Isaiah 29:10)

Conceive chaff and give birth to stubble. *As for your spirit,* fire will devour you. (Isaiah 33:11)

[6] (f) *Living in subjection to hell.*

I will make *the unclean spirit* depart from the land. (Zechariah 13:2)

When *an unclean spirit* goes out of someone, it wanders through dry places, and then recruits seven *spirits worse* than itself, and they come in and live there. (Matthew 12:43, 44, 45)

Babylon has become a refuge for every *unclean spirit.* (Revelation 18:2)

[7] (g) Then there are the hellish spirits by whom we are tormented: Matthew 8:16; 10:1; 12:43, 44, 45; Mark 1:23–28; 9:17–29; Luke 4:33, 36; 6:17, 18; 7:21; 8:2, 29; 9:39, 42, 55; 11:24, 25, 26; 13:11; Revelation 13:15; 16:13, 14.

49 3. *"Spirit" means the life of those who have been regenerated, which is called spiritual life.*

Jesus said, "Unless you have been born of water and *the spirit* you cannot enter the kingdom of God." (John 3:5)

I will give you a new heart and *a new spirit.* I will put *my spirit* within you and cause you to walk in my statutes. (Ezekiel 36:26, 27)

God will give a new heart and *a new spirit.* (Ezekiel 11:19)

Create a clean heart in me, O God, and renew *a strong spirit* within me. Bring back to me the joy of your salvation, and let *a willing spirit* uphold me. (Psalms 51:10, 11, 12)

Make yourselves a new heart and a new *spirit.* Why will you die, O house of Israel? (Ezekiel 18:31)

You send out your *spirit,* and they are created; you renew the face of the earth. (Psalms 104:30)

The hour is coming, and is now here, when true worshipers will worship the Father in *spirit* and in truth. (John 4:23)

Jehovah God gives soul to the people and *spirit* to those who are walking on [the earth]. (Isaiah 42:5)

Jehovah forms *the human spirit* within us. (Zechariah 12:1)

With my soul I have awaited you in the night; *with my spirit* within me I have awaited you in the morning. (Isaiah 26:9)

On that day Jehovah will become *a spirit of judgment* to the one who sits in judgment. (Isaiah 28:6)

My spirit has rejoiced in God my Savior. (Luke 1:47)

They have given rest to *my spirit* in the land of the north. (Zechariah 6:8)

Into your hand I commit *my spirit;* you have redeemed me. (Psalms 31:5)

There was not one, even among the remnant who had *spirit.* (Malachi 2:15)

After three and a half days the *spirit of life* from God entered the two witnesses who had been killed by the beast. (Revelation 11:11)

I, Jehovah, form the mountains and create *the spirit.* (Amos 4:13)

O God, the God of *the spirits* for all flesh . . . (Numbers 16:22; 27:18)

I will pour *a spirit from on high* upon the house of David and upon the inhabitants of Jerusalem. (Zechariah 12:10)

. . . even until he has poured out upon us *a spirit from on high.* (Isaiah 32:15)

I will pour out waters upon those who are thirsty and streams upon the dry land; *I will pour out my spirit* upon your seed. (Isaiah 44:3)

I will pour out *my spirit* upon all flesh; also upon my male and female servants *I will pour out spirit* in those days. (Joel 2:28, 29)

To pour out *the spirit* means to regenerate, as does to give a new heart and a new spirit.

[2] *"Spirit"* refers to the spiritual life of people who have been genuinely humbled.

I dwell in a crushed and *humble spirit,* to bring to life the *spirit of the humble* and to bring to life the heart of the crushed. (Isaiah 57:15)

The sacrifices of God are *a broken spirit;* God will not scorn a crushed and broken heart. (Psalms 51:17)

He will give the oil of joy in place of mourning, and a garment of praise in place of a confined *spirit.* (Isaiah 61:3)

. . . a woman abandoned and *afflicted in spirit.* (Isaiah 54:6)

Blessed are the *poor in spirit,* because theirs is the kingdom of the heavens. (Matthew 5:3)

50   4. *Where "spirit" is used in speaking of the Lord, it means his divine life and therefore the Lord himself.*

The one whom the Father sent speaks the words of God; without limit God has given him *the spirit.* The Father loves the Son and has given all things into his hand. (John 3:34, 35)

A shoot will go forth from the trunk of Jesse; *the spirit of Jehovah* will rest upon him, *the spirit of wisdom* and intelligence, *the spirit of counsel* and strength. (Isaiah 11:1, 2)

I have put *my spirit* upon him; he will bring forth judgment to the nations. (Isaiah 42:1)

He will come [to us] as a narrow river; in him *the spirit of Jehovah* will bring [us] a sign. Then he will come to Zion as the Redeemer. (Isaiah 59:19, 20)

The spirit of the Lord Jehovih is upon me; Jehovah has anointed me to bring good news to the poor. (Isaiah 61:1; Luke 4:18)

Jesus perceived *in his spirit* that they were having these thoughts within themselves. (Mark 2:8)

Jesus rejoiced *in his spirit* and said . . . (Luke 10:21)

Jesus was troubled *in his spirit.* (John 13:21)

Jesus sighed deeply *in his spirit.* (Mark 8:12)

[2] *"Spirit"* [stands] *for Jehovah himself or the Lord.*

God is *a spirit.* (John 4:24)

Who directed *the spirit* of Jehovah, or who was the man of his counsel? (Isaiah 40:13)

The spirit of Jehovah led them by means of the hand of Moses. (Isaiah 63:11, 12, 14)

Where shall I go from *your spirit,* and where shall I flee? (Psalms 139:7)

Jehovah said, "[Zerubbabel] will accomplish this not by might but by *my spirit.*" (Zechariah 4:6)

They angered the *spirit of* his *holiness;* therefore he turned into an enemy for them. ([Isaiah 63:10]; Psalms 106:33)

My spirit will not contend with humankind forever, because humankind is flesh. (Genesis 6:3)

I will not dispute forever, because *the spirit* would fail in my presence. (Isaiah 57:16)

Blasphemy against the *Holy Spirit* will not be forgiven, but someone who says a word against the Son of Humanity will be forgiven. (Matthew 12:31, 32; Mark 3:28, 29, 30; Luke 12:10)

Blasphemy against the Holy Spirit is blasphemy against the Lord's divine nature. Blasphemy against the Son of Humanity is something contrary to the Word, understanding its meaning differently. The Son of Humanity is the Lord as the Word, as already explained [§§23–28].

5. *When "spirit" is used in speaking of the Lord, it means specifically the life of his wisdom, which is divine truth.*

51

I tell you *the truth.* It is to your advantage that I go away. If I do not go away, *the Comforter* will not come to you; but if I go away, I will send him to you. (John 16:7)

When he, *the Spirit of Truth,* has come, he will guide you into all *truth.* He will not speak on his own authority, but will say whatever he has heard. (John 16:13)

He will glorify me, because he will take *of what is mine* and declare it to you. All things that the Father has are mine. That is why I said that he will take *of what is mine* and declare it to you. (John 16:14, 15)

I will ask the Father to give you another *Comforter, the Spirit of Truth.* The world cannot receive him, because it does not see him or know him; but you know him, because he dwells among you and will be in you. I will not leave you orphans; I am coming to you. You will see me. (John 14:16, 17, 18, 19)

When *the Comforter* comes, whom I will send to you from the Father, *the Spirit of Truth,* he will testify concerning me. (John 15:26)

Jesus cried out, saying, "If any are thirsty, they must come to me and drink. As the Scripture says, from the bellies of those who believe in me will flow rivers of living water." He said this concerning *the Spirit* that those who believed in him would receive. *There was not the Holy Spirit yet because Jesus was not yet glorified.* (John 7:37, 38, 39)

Jesus breathed on the disciples and said, "Receive *the Holy Spirit.*" (John 20:22)

[2] We can see that the Lord meant himself by the Comforter, the Spirit of Truth, and the Holy Spirit from these words of the Lord, *that the world did not yet know him*—that is, they did not yet know the Lord. Further, when he said that he would send him, he added,

I will not leave you orphans; I am coming to you, and you will see me. (John 14:16–19, 26, 28)

And in another passage,

Behold, I am with you all the days, even to the close of the age. (Matthew 28:20)

And when Thomas said, "We do not know where you are going," Jesus said, "*I am the way and the truth*" (John 14:5, 6).

[3] Because the Spirit of Truth or the Holy Spirit is the same as the Lord, who is the truth itself, it also says "*There was not the Holy Spirit yet because Jesus was not yet glorified*" (John 7:39). This is because after his glorification or full union with the Father, which was accomplished by his suffering on the cross, the Lord was then divine wisdom itself and divine truth—therefore the Holy Spirit.

The reason the Lord breathed on the disciples and said "Receive the Holy Spirit" was that all of heaven's breathing originates with the Lord. Angels breathe just as we do, and their hearts beat. Their breathing depends on their acceptance of divine wisdom from the Lord and their heartbeat or pulse depends on their acceptance of divine love from the Lord. This will be explained in its proper place.

[4] From the following passages we can clearly see that the Holy Spirit is divine truth that comes from the Lord:

When they hand you over to the synagogues, do not worry about what you are going to say. *The Holy Spirit* will teach you in that very hour what you should say. (Luke 12:11, 12; 21:14; Mark 13:11)

Jehovah said, "*My spirit,* which is upon you, and my words, which I have placed in your mouth, shall not depart from your mouth." (Isaiah 59:21)

A shoot will go forth from the trunk of Jesse. He will strike the earth with the rod of his mouth, and *with the spirit of his lips* he will slay the ungodly. *Truth* will be a belt around his hips. (Isaiah 11:1, 4, 5)

Now he has commanded with his mouth and *his spirit* has gathered them. (Isaiah 34:16)

Those who worship God must worship *in spirit and in truth*. (John 4:24)

It is the spirit that gives life—the flesh is of no benefit. The words that I speak to you *are spirit and are life*. (John 6:63)

John said, "I am baptizing you with water into repentance, but the one who is to come after me will baptize you with *the Holy Spirit and with fire*." (Matthew 3:11; Mark 1:8; Luke 3:16)

To baptize with the Holy Spirit and with fire is to regenerate by means of the divine truth that produces faith and the divine goodness that produces love [within us].

When Jesus was being baptized, the heavens were opened and he saw *the Holy Spirit* coming down like a dove. (Matthew 3:16; Mark 1:10; Luke 3:21; John 1:32, 33)

A dove represents purification and regeneration by means of divine truth.

[5] When "the Holy Spirit" is used in speaking of the Lord it means his divine life and therefore himself, and specifically it means the life of his wisdom, which is called divine truth; therefore the spirit of the prophets, which is also called the Holy Spirit, means divine truth that comes from the Lord. This is the case in the following passages:

. . . what *the Spirit* says to the churches. (Revelation 2:7, 11, 29; 3:1, 6, 13, 22)

The seven lamps of fire burning before the throne are *the seven spirits of God*. (Revelation 4:5)

In the midst of the elders stood a Lamb, having seven eyes, which are *the seven spirits of God* sent out into all the earth. (Revelation 5:6)

The lamps of fire and the eyes of the Lord mean divine truths, and seven means what is holy.

. . . says *the Spirit*, "so that they may rest from their labors." (Revelation 14:13)

The Spirit and the bride say, "Come." (Revelation 22:17)

They made their hearts diamond-hard so that they would not hear the law or the words that *Jehovah* sent *by his spirit* through the hand of the prophets. (Zechariah 7:12)

The spirit of Elijah came upon Elisha. (2 Kings 2:15)

John went before [the Lord] *in the spirit* and power of Elijah. (Luke 1:17)

Elizabeth was filled *with the Holy Spirit* and prophesied. (Luke 1:41)

Zechariah was filled *with the Holy Spirit* and prophesied. (Luke 1:67)

David said by *the Holy Spirit,* "The Lord said to my Lord, 'Sit at my right hand.'" (Mark 12:36)

The testimony of Jesus is the spirit of prophecy. (Revelation 19:10)

Since, then, the Holy Spirit means specifically the Lord's divine wisdom and therefore his divine truth, we can see why it is that people say of the Holy Spirit that it *enlightens, teaches,* and *inspires.*

52   6. *Jehovah himself—that is, the Lord—spoke the Word through prophets.* We read of the prophets that they had *visions* and that *Jehovah talked with them.* When they had visions, they were not focused on their bodies but on the spirit, in which state they saw things of a heavenly nature. When Jehovah talked with them, though, they were conscious of their bodies and heard Jehovah speaking.

We need to draw a clear distinction between these two states. In a *visionary* state, the eyes of their spirit were open and the eyes of their body were closed; and at such times they seemed to themselves to be taken from place to place while their bodies stayed where they were. Ezekiel, Zechariah, and Daniel were in this state at times, and so was John when he wrote the Book of Revelation. They were then said to be in *a vision* or in *the spirit.* In fact, Ezekiel says,

The spirit lifted me up and brought me back into Chaldea, to the captivity, in *a vision from God,* in *the spirit of God.* In this way *the vision* that I saw came over me. (Ezekiel 11:1, 24)

He says that the spirit lifted him up and that he heard an earthquake and other things behind him (Ezekiel 3:12, 14). He also said that the spirit lifted him up between earth and heaven and took him off into Jerusalem in *visions from God,* and he saw abominations (Ezekiel 8:3 and following).

That is why (again in a vision of God or in the spirit) Ezekiel saw the four beasts that were angel guardians (chapters 1 and 10), and he saw a new earth and a new temple with the angel measuring them, as we are told in chapters 40–48. He says in chapter 40, verse 2, that he was then in visions from God; and in chapter 43, verse 5, he says that the spirit lifted him up at that time.

The same thing happened with *Zechariah.* There was an angel inwardly present with him when he saw a man riding among myrtle trees (Zechariah 1:8 and following); when he saw four horns and then a man with a measuring line in his hand (Zechariah 1:18; 2:1); when he saw Joshua the high priest (Zechariah 3:1 and following); when he saw a lampstand and two olive trees (Zechariah 4:1 and following); when he saw a flying scroll and a measuring basket (Zechariah 5:1, 6); and when he saw four chariots coming from between two mountains, along with horses (Zechariah 6:1 and following).

Daniel was in the same kind of state when he saw four beasts come up from the sea (Daniel 7:3) and when he saw battles between a ram and a goat (Daniel 8:1 and following).

We read in Daniel 7:1, 2, 7, 13; 8:2; 10:1, 7, 8 that he saw these things in visions. We read in Daniel 9:21 that he saw the angel Gabriel in a vision and talked with him.

Much the same happened with John when he wrote the Book of Revelation. He says that he was *in the spirit* on the Lord's day (Revelation 1:10), that he was carried away *in the spirit* into the wilderness (17:3), to a high mountain *in the spirit* (21:10), that he saw horses *in a vision* (9:17), and elsewhere that *he saw* what he described, being therefore in the spirit or in a vision (1:2; 4:1; 5:1; 6:1; and in the particular chapters that follow).

As for the Word itself, it does not say in the prophets that they spoke it from the Holy Spirit but that they spoke it from Jehovah, Jehovah Sabaoth, or the Lord Jehovih, since it says that *the Word of Jehovah came to me,* that *Jehovah spoke to me,* and very often, *Jehovah said* and *the saying of Jehovah.* Since the Lord is Jehovah, then (as already explained [§§38, 45]), the whole Word was spoken by him.

So that no one will doubt that this is the case, I want to list the places in Jeremiah alone where it says *the Word of Jehovah came to me, Jehovah spoke to me, Jehovah said,* and *the saying of Jehovah,* which are the following: Jeremiah 1:4, 11, 12, 13, 14, 19; 2:1, 2, 3, 4, 5, 9, 19, 22, 29, 31; 3:1, 6, 10, 12, 14, 16; 4:1, 3, 9, 17, 27; 5:11, 14, 18, 22, 29; 6:6, 9, 12, 15, 16, 21, 22; 7:1, 3, 11, 13, 19, 20, 21; 8:1, 3, 12, 13; 9:3, 6, 7, 9, 13, 15, 17, 22, 23, 24, 25; 10:1, 2, 18; 11:1, 6, 9, 11; 12:14, 17; 13:1, 6, 9, 11, 12, 13, 14, 15, 25; 14:1, 10, 14, 15; 15:1, 2, 3, 6, 11, 19, 20; 16:1, 3, 5, 9, 14, 16; 17:5, 19, 20, 21, 24; 18:1, 5, 6, 11, 13; 19:1, 3, 6, 12, 15; 20:4; 21:1, 4, 7, 8, 11, 12; 22:2, 5, 6, 11, 16, 18, 24, 29,

30; 23:2, 5, 7, 12, 15, 24, 29, 31, 38; 24:3, 5, 8; 25:1, 3, 7, 8, 9, 15, 27, 29, 32; 26:1, 2, 18; 27:1, 2, 4, 8, 11, 16, 19, 21, 22; 28:2, 12, 14, 16; 29:4, 8, 9, 19, 20, 21, 25, 30, 31, 32; 30:1, 2, 3, 4, 5, 8, 10, 11, 12, 17, 18; 31:1, 2, 7, 10, 15, 16, 17, 23, 27, 28, 31, 32, 33, 34, 35, 36, 37, 38; 32:1, 6, 14, 15, 25, 26, 28, 30, 36, 42; 33:1, 2, 4, 10, 11, 12, 13, 17, 19, 20, 23, 25; 34:1, 2, 4, 8, 12, 13, 17, 22; 35:1, 13, 17, 18, 19; 36:1, 6, 27, 29, 30; 37:6, 7, 9; 38:2, 3, 17; 39:15, 16, 17, 18; 40:1; 42:7, 9, 15, 18, 19; 43:8, 10; 44:1, 2, 7, 11, 24, 25, 26, 30; 45:1, 2, 5; 46:1, 23, 25, 28; 47:1; 48:1, 8, 12, 30, 35, 38, 40, 43, 44, 47; 49:2, 5, 6, 7, 12, 13, 16, 18, 26, 28, 30, 32, 35, 37, 38, 39; 50:1, 4, 10, 18, 20, 21, 30, 31, 33, 35, 40; 51:25, 33, 36, 39, 52, 58.

These are from Jeremiah alone. It says things like this in all the other prophets and does not say that the Holy Spirit spoke or that Jehovah spoke to them through the Holy Spirit.

54　　We can now see from this that *Jehovah,* who is *the Lord from eternity,* spoke through the prophets and that where it speaks of *the Holy Spirit,* it is he himself.

Therefore, *God is one in person and in essence, and he is the Lord.*

The Athanasian Statement of Faith Agrees with the Truth, Provided That We Understand It to Be Referring Not to "a Trinity of Persons" but to "a Trinity within One Person," Who Is the Lord

55　　THE reason Christians have acknowledged three divine persons and therefore something like three gods is that there is a trinity within the Lord; one element is called the Father, the second the Son, and the third the Holy Spirit. Further, these three are distinguished from each other in the Word, just as the soul and the body and what comes forth from them are distinguished from each other, even though they are one.

It is the nature of the Word in its literal meaning to distinguish things that are one as though they were not one. That is why Jehovah, who is the Lord from eternity, is sometimes called Jehovah, sometimes Jehovah Sabaoth, sometimes God, sometimes the Lord, as well as Creator, Savior, Redeemer, and Maker, and even Shaddai. Then too, the human nature that he took on in the world is called Jesus, Christ, Messiah, Son of God, Son of Humanity; and in the Word of the Old Testament it is called God, the Holy One of Israel, Jehovah's Anointed, King, Prince, Counselor, Angel, and David.

[2] Now, since it is typical of the Word in its literal meaning to name many when in fact they are one, Christians—the first of whom were simple individuals who took everything that was said literally—divided Divinity into three persons. This was tolerated because they were simple people. However, they took this in such a way that they also believed *the Son* to be infinite, uncreate, almighty, God, and Lord, completely equal to the Father; and they also believed that in essence, majesty, and glory, and therefore in divinity they were not two or three but one.

[3] If people believe this in a simple way, because this is what they were taught, and do not convince themselves of three gods but make the three into one, after death they are taught by the Lord through angels that he is that very One and that Trinity, a belief accepted by everyone who comes into heaven. This is because no one can be allowed into heaven who thinks in terms of three gods, no matter how much she or he verbally professes one God. The life of all heaven and the wisdom of all angels is based on the acknowledgment and consequent confession of one God, on a faith that this one God is also human, and on a belief that he is himself the Lord, who is at once God and a human being.

[4] We can see, then, that God allowed the first Christians to accept a teaching regarding three persons provided they also accepted at the same time a belief that the Lord is the infinite, almighty God and Jehovah. This was because if they had not accepted this as well, it would have been all over with the church, since the church is the church because of the Lord, and the eternal life of all comes from the Lord and from no one else.

[5] We can be quite sure that the church is the church because of the Lord simply from the fact that the whole Word, from beginning to end, is about the Lord alone (as already explained [§§1–7]), that we are to believe in him, and that those who do not believe in him do not have eternal life; instead, the wrath of God abides on them (John 3:36).

[6] Now, since we can all see within ourselves that if God is one, he is *one both in person and in essence* (really, no one thinks anything else or can think anything else when thinking that God is one), I should like at this point to bring in the whole doctrinal statement named for Athanasius and then show that everything it says is true, provided that we understand it to be referring to "a trinity within one person" rather than "a trinity of persons."

56 *The doctrinal statement* is this:

For all who want to be saved, it is necessary that they hold the catholic [other versions of the statement read "Christian"] faith. Unless they keep that faith whole and undefiled, without doubt they will perish everlastingly. And the catholic [or "Christian"] faith is this: That we worship one God in trinity, and trinity in unity, neither confounding the persons nor dividing the substance [or "essence"]. For there is one person of the Father, another of the Son, and another of the Holy Spirit. But the divinity of the Father, of the Son, and of the Holy Spirit is all one, the glory equal, the majesty coeternal. Such as the Father is, such is the Son, and such is the Holy Spirit. The Father is uncreate, the Son is uncreate, and the Holy Spirit is uncreate. The Father is infinite, the Son is infinite, and the Holy Spirit is infinite. The Father is eternal, the Son is eternal, and the Holy Spirit is eternal. And yet there are not three eternal beings but one eternal Being, as also there are not three infinite or three uncreated beings, but one uncreated and one infinite Being. So likewise the Father is almighty, the Son is almighty, and the Holy Spirit is almighty; and yet there are not three almighty beings, but one almighty Being. So the Father is God, the Son is God, and the Holy Spirit is God; and yet there are not three gods, but one God. So likewise the Father is Lord, the Son is Lord, and the Holy Spirit is Lord; and yet there are not three lords, but one Lord. For just as we are compelled by Christian truth to acknowledge each person by himself to be both God and Lord, so are we forbidden by the catholic religion to say that there are three gods or three lords [or "so in the Christian faith we cannot mention three gods or three lords"]. The Father is made by none, neither created nor begotten. The Son is from the Father alone, not made, nor created, but begotten. The Holy Spirit is from the Father and from the Son, neither made, nor created, nor begotten, but proceeding. So there is one Father, not three Fathers; one Son, not three Sons; one Holy Spirit, not three Holy Spirits. And in this trinity none is first or last; none is greatest or least; but all three persons are coeternal together, and coequal. So in all things, as said above, the unity in trinity and the trinity in unity is to be worshiped [or "three persons in one Divinity and one God in three persons is to be worshiped"]. So this is how we must think of the trinity if we want to be saved.

Furthermore, it is necessary to salvation that we also believe rightly in the Incarnation of our Lord Jesus Christ [or "that we firmly believe that our Lord is truly human"]. For the true faith is that we believe and confess that our Lord Jesus Christ, the Son of God, is God and a human being, God from the substance [or "essence"; others read "nature"] of the Father, begotten before the world; and human from the substance [or "nature"] of his mother, born in the world; perfect God and perfect human being, consisting of a rational soul and a human body; equal to the Father with respect to his divinity, and inferior to [or "less than"] the Father with respect to his humanity. Although he is God and a human being, yet he is not two, but one Christ; one, not by conversion of divinity into flesh, but by taking humanity into God [or "he is one, not because the divine nature was changed into the human nature but because the divine nature took the human nature into itself"]. One altogether; not by confusion [or "mixing"] of substance, but by unity of person [or "he is one altogether; not because the two natures were mixed but because he is one person"]. Therefore as the rational soul and the body is one human being, so God and a human being is one Christ; who suffered for our salvation, descended into hell, and rose again the third day from the dead. He ascended into heaven, and sits at the right hand of the Father Almighty. From there he will come to judge the living and the dead; at his Coming all will rise again with their bodies; and those who have done good will go into everlasting life and those who have done evil will go into everlasting fire.

We can see that this whole doctrinal statement is true right down to the individual words, provided that rather than "a trinity of persons" we understand it to be referring to "a trinity within one person," by rewriting it and substituting this latter trinity. The "trinity within one person" is this: *the divine nature of the Lord is the Father, the divine-human nature is the Son, and the emanating divine nature is the Holy Spirit.*

When we have this trinity in mind, then we can think of one God and also say "one God"; otherwise, we cannot help but think in terms of three gods. Can anyone fail to see this? Athanasius saw it, which is why these words were inserted into his doctrinal statement:

> For just as we are compelled by Christian truth to acknowledge each person by himself to be both God and Lord, so by the catholic religion or the Christian faith we cannot say or mention three gods or three lords.

This is like saying that even though Christian truth allows us to acknowledge or think in terms of three gods or three lords, the Christian faith allows us to say or mention only one God or one Lord. Yet it is acknowledgment and thought that unite us to the Lord and to heaven, not speech alone.

Further, no one understands how a divine nature that is one can be divided into three persons, each of which is God. That is, the divine nature is not divisible, and making the three one because of their essence or substance does not get rid of the idea of three gods. All it does is give the impression that they agree with each other.

58 If this whole doctrinal statement is rewritten as follows, [the point just made] becomes clear, that it is true right down to the individual words, provided that rather than a "trinity of persons" we understand it to be referring to a "trinity within one person":

> For all who want to be saved, it is necessary that they hold the Christian faith. And the Christian faith is this: That we worship one God in trinity, and trinity in unity, neither confounding the three aspects within his person nor dividing his essence. The three aspects within him as one person are what are referred to as the Father, the Son, and the Holy Spirit. The divinity of the Father, of the Son, and of the Holy Spirit is all one, the glory and majesty equal. Such as the Father is, such is the Son, and such is the Holy Spirit. The Father is uncreate, the Son is uncreate, and the Holy Spirit is uncreate. The Father is infinite, the Son is infinite, and the Holy Spirit is infinite. And yet there are not three infinite or three uncreated beings, but one uncreated and one infinite Being. So likewise the Father is almighty, the Son is almighty, and the Holy Spirit is almighty; and yet there are not three almighty beings, but one almighty Being. So the Father is God, the Son is God, and the Holy Spirit is God; and yet there are not three gods, but one God. So likewise the Father is Lord, the Son is Lord, and the Holy Spirit is Lord; and yet there are not three lords, but one Lord. Now, as in Christian truth we acknowledge three aspects in one person who is God and

Lord, so in Christian faith we can say one God and one Lord. The Father is made by none, neither created nor begotten. The Son is from the Father alone, not made, nor created, but begotten. The Holy Spirit is from the Father and from the Son, neither made, nor created, nor begotten, but proceeding. So there is one Father, not three Fathers; one Son, not three Sons; one Holy Spirit, not three Holy Spirits. And in this trinity none is greatest or least; they are absolutely equal. So in all things, as said above, the unity in trinity and the trinity in unity is to be worshiped.

This deals with what this doctrinal statement has to say about the trinity and unity of God. There then follow points about the Lord's taking on of a human nature in the world, which is called incarnation. These too are true in every way, provided we clearly differentiate between the human nature from the mother that the Lord was conscious of when he was in states of being brought low or being emptied out and suffered trials and the cross, and the human nature from the Father that he was conscious of when he was in states of being glorified or united [to the divine nature]. That is, in the world the Lord took on a human nature that was conceived by Jehovah, who is the Lord from eternity, and was born of the Virgin Mary. This means he had a divine nature and a human nature—the divine from his own divine nature from eternity, and the human from his mother Mary in time. He put off this latter nature, though, and put on the divine human nature. It is this human nature that is called "the divine human nature" and in the Word is meant by "the Son of God." So when the points that come next in the statement about the Incarnation are understood to refer to the maternal human nature that he was conscious of in his states of being brought low, and the statements that follow those [are understood to be] about the divine-human nature that he was conscious of in his states of being glorified, then everything fits together.

The following things that come next in the statement are accurate in regard to the maternal human nature he was conscious of in his states of being brought low.

> Jesus Christ is God and a human being, God from the substance of the Father, and human from the substance of his mother, born in the world; perfect God and perfect human being, consisting of a rational soul and a human body; equal to the Father with respect to his divinity, and less than the Father with respect to his humanity.

And this,

> That human nature was not converted into a divine nature or mixed with it but was put off, and a divine-human nature was put on in its place.

The things that follow those in the statement are accurate in regard to the human-divine nature that he was conscious of in his states of being glorified and in which he is now and will be to eternity.

> Although our Lord Jesus Christ, the Son of God, is God and a human being, yet he is not two, but one Christ. He is one altogether, because he is one person. Therefore as the soul and the body make one human being, so God and a human being is one Christ.

60 The assertions in this doctrinal statement that God and a human being in the Lord are not two but one person, and are one altogether the way the soul and the body are one, show through clearly in many of the things that the Lord himself said; for example, that the Father and he are one [John 10:30], that all that is the Father's is his, and all that is his is the Father's [John 17:10], that he is in the Father and the Father is in him [John 14:10], that all things have been given into his hand [John 13:3], that he has all power [Matthew 28:18], that he is the God of heaven and earth [Matthew 28:18], that those who believe in him have eternal life [John 6:47], and so on; also that both the divine nature and the human nature were raised into heaven and that in both respects he sits at the right hand of God [Mark 16:19] (that is, that he is almighty), and more passages from the Word concerning his divine-human nature that have been cited above [§§29–36] in ample number, all of which testify that *God is one both in person and in essence, in whom there is a trinity, and that that God is the Lord.*

61 The reason these facts about the Lord are now being made known for the first time is that in Revelation 21 and 22 it was foretold that a new church would be established by the Lord at the close of the former one, a church in which this teaching would be first and foremost. This church is what is meant in Revelation by the New Jerusalem [Revelation 3:12; 21:2] into which only those who recognize the Lord alone as God of heaven and earth can enter. This I can proclaim: that the whole heaven acknowledges the Lord alone, and anyone who does not share in this acknowledgment is not allowed into heaven. The fact of the matter is that heaven is heaven because of the Lord. That very acknowledgment, made in the spirit of love and faith, causes the people there to be in the Lord and the Lord to be in them. This is what the Lord himself is telling us in John:

> On that day you will know that I am in my Father, and you are in me, and I am in you. (John 14:20)

And again,

> Abide in me, and I [will abide] in you. I am the vine; you are the branches. Those who abide in me and in whom I abide bear much fruit, because without me you cannot do anything. If any do not abide in me, they are cast out. (John 15:4, 5, 6; and 17:22, 23)

[2] The reason this has not been seen in the Word before is that if it had been seen too early it would not have been accepted. That is, the Last Judgment had not been carried out yet, and before that happened the power of hell was stronger than the power of heaven. We are in between heaven and hell, so if this had been seen too early, the Devil (that is, hell) would have snatched it out of our hearts and then proceeded to profane it. This state of hell's power was decisively broken by the Last Judgment that has now been carried out. Since then—now, that is—anyone who wants to be enlightened and wise can be: see what is written about this in *Heaven and Hell* 589–596 and 597–603 as well as the booklet *Last Judgment* 65–72 and 73–74.

The New Jerusalem in the Book of Revelation Means a New Church

IN the Book of Revelation we find a description of the state of the **62** Christian church as it would be at its close and as it now is. We are told that those people from that church who were meant by the false prophet,

the dragon, the whore, and the beasts were cast into hell. After this—
after the completion of the Last Judgment, that is—it says the following:

> I saw a new heaven and a new earth, because the first heaven and the
> first earth had passed away. Then I, John, saw the holy city Jerusalem,
> coming down from God out of heaven. And I heard a loud voice from
> heaven saying, "Behold, the tabernacle of God is among people, and
> he will dwell with them, and they will be his people. And God himself
> will be with them and be their God." The one who sat on the throne
> said, "Behold, I am making all things new." And he said to me, "Write,
> because these words are true and faithful." (Revelation 21:1, 2, 3, 5)

The new heaven and the new earth that John saw after the first heaven
and the first earth had passed away do not mean a new sky like the one
we can see with our eyes, full of air and stars, or a new earth for us to live
on, but a new kind of church in the spiritual world and a new kind of
church in this earthly world.

[2] Because the Lord, when he was in this world, made a new kind of
church in both the spiritual and the earthly worlds, it says similar things
in the prophets, namely, that a new heaven and a new earth were going
to come into being at that time, as we find in Isaiah 65:17; 66:22; and
elsewhere—which cannot therefore be understood to refer to the sky that
we can see with our eyes and the earth that we live on.

"The spiritual world" means the world where angels and spirits live,
and "the earthly world" means the world where we are living. On the recent
founding of a new kind of church in the spiritual world and the even-
tual founding of a new kind of church in the earthly world, there is
some information in the booklet *Last Judgment* [§§1–5] and more in the
supplement to that work.

63   The holy city Jerusalem means that new church in regard to its teachings. That is why it was seen coming down from God out of heaven,
because the only source of genuinely true teaching is through heaven from
the Lord.

It is because the city New Jerusalem means the church in regard to
its teachings that it says "prepared as a bride adorned for her husband"
(Revelation 21:2) and then,

> One of the seven angels came to me and talked with me, saying,
> "Come, I will show you the bride, the wife of the Lamb." And he car-
> ried me away in the spirit to a high mountain, and showed me the
> great city, the holy Jerusalem, coming down out of heaven from God.
> (Revelation 21:9, 10)

It is common knowledge that the bride and wife mean the church and the Bridegroom and Husband mean the Lord. The church is the bride when it is willing to receive the Lord and is the wife when it does receive him. We can see that the Husband means the Lord in this passage because it says "the bride, the wife of the Lamb."

The reason Jerusalem in the Word means the church in regard to its teachings is that that was the only place in the land of Canaan where the Temple was, where the altar was, where sacrifices were performed, and therefore where there was actual worship of God. That was also why the three annual feasts were celebrated there and why every male in the whole land was commanded to go there. This is why Jerusalem means the church in regard to worship and therefore also the church in regard to its teachings, since worship is defined by teachings and carried out in accord with them. It is also because the Lord was in Jerusalem and taught in its Temple and afterward glorified his human nature there.

Moreover, in the Word as spiritually understood a city means a body of teaching, so a holy city means a body of teaching based on divine truth that comes from the Lord.[a]

[2] We can also see that Jerusalem means a church in regard to its teachings from other passages in the Word, such as this in *Isaiah:*

> For Zion's sake I will not be silent and for Jerusalem's sake I will not rest until her justice goes forth like radiance and her salvation burns like a lamp. Then the nations will see your justice and all monarchs will see your glory, and a new name will be given you that the mouth of Jehovah will utter. And you will be a crown of beauty in the hand of Jehovah and a diadem of the kingdom in the hand of your God. Jehovah will be well pleased with you and your land will be married. Behold, your salvation will come. See, his reward is with him. And they will call them a holy people, the redeemed of Jehovah; and you will be called a city sought out, not deserted. (Isaiah 62:1, 2, 3, 4, 11, 12)

This whole chapter is about the Lord's Coming and about the new church that he is about to establish. This is the new church meant by the Jerusalem that will be given a new name that the mouth of Jehovah will utter

---

a. A city in the Word means the teachings of a church and of a religion: see *Secrets of Heaven* 402, 2712, 2943, 3216, 4492, 4493. The gate of a city means the teachings through which we come into the church. 2943, 4477. That is why the elders sat in the gate of the city and gave judgment: 2943. Going out of the gate means departing from the teachings: 4492, 4493. Representations of cities and palaces appear in heaven when angels are discussing specific teachings: 3216.

and that will be a crown of beauty in the hand of Jehovah and a diadem of the kingdom in the hand of God, with which Jehovah will be well pleased, and which will be called a city sought out, not deserted. This cannot mean the Jerusalem inhabited by the Jewish people at the time the Lord came into the world, because this was the opposite in all respects, and might more properly be called "Sodom," as it is in Revelation 11:8, Isaiah 3:9, Jeremiah 23:14, Ezekiel 16:46, 48. [3] Another passage from *Isaiah:*

> Behold, I am creating a new heaven and a new earth; the former ones will not be remembered. Be glad and rejoice forever in what I am creating. Behold, I am going to create Jerusalem as a rejoicing and her people as a gladness, so that I may rejoice over Jerusalem and be glad about my people. Then the wolf and the lamb will feed together; they will do no evil in all my holy mountain. (Isaiah 65:17, 18, 19, 25)

This chapter too is about the Lord's Coming and the church that he is going to establish—a church that was not established among people in Jerusalem but among people who were outside it. This church, then, is meant by the Jerusalem that would be a rejoicing for the Lord and whose people will be a gladness for him, and where the wolf and the lamb will feed together, and where they will do no evil.

Here it is also saying, as it does in the Book of Revelation, that the Lord is going to create a new heaven and a new earth, meaning much the same thing; and it also says that he is going to create Jerusalem. [4] Another passage from *Isaiah:*

> Wake up! Wake up! Put on your strength, O Zion. Put on your beautiful garments, O Jerusalem, holy city. No more will the uncircumcised or the unclean come into you. Shake yourself from the dust, rise up, and sit, Jerusalem. The people will acknowledge my name on that day, because I am the one saying, "Here I am!" Jehovah has comforted his people; he has redeemed Jerusalem. (Isaiah 52:1, 2, 6, 9)

This chapter too is about the Lord's Coming and the church that he is going to establish. So the Jerusalem into which the uncircumcised or the unclean will no longer come, and which the Lord will redeem, means the church; and Jerusalem the holy city means the church's teachings that come from the Lord. [5] In Zephaniah:

> Rejoice, O daughter of Zion! Be glad with all your heart, O daughter of Jerusalem! The King of Israel is in your midst. Do not fear evil

anymore. He will be glad over you with joy; he will rest in your love; he will rejoice over you with singing. I will give you a name and praise among all the peoples of the earth. (Zephaniah 3:14, 15, 16, 17, 20)

Again, this is about the Lord and the church from him, the church over which the King of Israel (who is the Lord) will rejoice with singing and be glad with joy, in whose love he will be at rest, and to whom he will give a name and praise among all the peoples of the earth. [6] In Isaiah:

Thus says Jehovah your Redeemer and your Maker, who says to Jerusalem, "You will be inhabited," and to the cities of Judah, "You will be built." (Isaiah 44:24, 26)

And in Daniel:

Know and understand: from [the time] the word goes forth that Jerusalem must be restored and built until [the time of] Messiah the Leader will be seven weeks. (Daniel 9:25)

We can see that here too Jerusalem means the church because this latter was restored and built up by the Lord, but Jerusalem, the capital city of the Jewish people, was not.

[7] Jerusalem means the church that comes from the Lord also in the following passages. In Zechariah:

Thus says Jehovah: "I will return to Zion and dwell in the midst of Jerusalem. Jerusalem will be called the city of truth, and the mountain of Jehovah Sabaoth will be called the holy mountain." (Zechariah 8:3; see also 8:20–23)

In Joel:

Then you will know that I am Jehovah your God, dwelling on Zion, my holy mountain. Jerusalem will be holy. And on that day it will happen that the mountains will drip with new wine and the hills will flow with milk; and Jerusalem will abide from generation to generation. (Joel 3:17–21)

In Isaiah:

On that day the branch of Jehovah will be beautiful and glorious. And it will happen that those remaining in Zion and those left in Jerusalem will be called holy—all who are written as alive in Jerusalem. (Isaiah 4:2, 3)

In Micah:

> At the very last of days the mountain of the house of Jehovah will be established on the top of the mountains. Teaching will go forth from Zion and the word of Jehovah from Jerusalem. To you the former kingdom will come, the kingdom of the daughter of Jerusalem. (Micah 4:1, 2, 8)

In Jeremiah:

> At that time they will call Jerusalem the throne of Jehovah, and all nations will gather at Jerusalem because of the name of Jehovah. They will no longer follow the stubbornness of their own evil heart. (Jeremiah 3:17)

In Isaiah:

> Look upon Zion, the city of our appointed feasts! Your eyes will see Jerusalem as a peaceful abode and as a tabernacle that will not be taken down; its tent pegs will never be removed and not one of its cords will be torn away. (Isaiah 33:20)

There are other passages elsewhere, such as Isaiah 24:23; 37:32; 66:10–14; Zechariah 12:3, 6, 9, 10; 14:8, 11, 12, 21; Malachi 3:2, 4; Psalms 122:1–7; 137:4, 5, 6.

[8] As for Jerusalem in these passages meaning the church that the Lord was going to establish and that has in fact been established, and not the Jerusalem in the land of Canaan that was inhabited by Jews, this too we can tell from the places in the Word where this latter city is described as totally lost and as destined for destruction, passages such as Jeremiah 5:1; 6:6, 7; 7:17, 18, and following; 8:6, 7, 8, and following; 9:10, 11, 13, and following; 13:9, 10, 14; 14:16; Lamentations 1:8, 9, 17; Ezekiel 4:1 to the end; 5:9 to the end; 12:18, 19; 15:6, 7, 8; 16:1–63; 23:1–49; Matthew 23:37, 39; Luke 19:41–44; 21:20, 21, 22; 23:28, 29, 30; and in many other places.

65 It says in the Book of Revelation, *a new heaven and a new earth* [Revelation 21:1], and after that, *Behold, I am making all things new* [Revelation 21:5]. This means simply that in the church that is now about to be established by the Lord, *there will be a new body of teaching* that did not exist in the former church. The reason it did not exist is that if it had existed it would not have been accepted. The Last Judgment had not yet been carried out, and until that happened the power of hell was stronger than the power of heaven. Consequently, if the Lord had given the new body of teaching too early, it would not have lasted with us; and even today it does not last except with people who turn to the Lord alone and acknowledge him as the God of heaven and earth (see §61 above).

This same teaching had in fact already been given in the Word, but since the church changed into Babylon not long after its establishment—and then, among some, into Philistia—this teaching could not be seen in the Word. This is because a church sees the Word only through the lens of its own religious principles and teachings.

The new principles that are in this booklet are, in general terms, the following:

1. God is one in person and in essence, and is the Lord.
2. The whole Sacred Scripture is about him alone.
3. He came into the world to subdue the hells and to glorify his human nature. He accomplished these two goals by allowing himself to undergo trials; he accomplished them fully by the last of these trials, which was the suffering on the cross. By this means he became Redeemer and Savior, and by this means he alone has merit and justice.
4. He fulfilled all of the law, meaning that he fulfilled all of the Word.
5. He did not take away our sins by his suffering on the cross, but he did carry them like a prophet—that is, he suffered in order to be a representation of how the church had abused the Word.
6. The imputation of merit is nothing unless we understand it to be the forgiveness of sins after repentance.

These principles have been presented in this booklet. In forthcoming works—on Sacred Scripture, on teachings about life, on faith, and on divine love and wisdom—there will be more that is new

BIOGRAPHICAL NOTE

Biographical Note

EMANUEL SWEDENBORG (1688–1772) was born Emanuel Swedberg (or Svedberg) in Stockholm, Sweden, on January 29, 1688 (Julian calendar). He was the third of the nine children of Jesper Swedberg (1653–1735) and Sara Behm (1666–1696). At the age of eight he lost his mother. After the death of his only older brother ten days later, he became the oldest living son. In 1697 his father married Sara Bergia (1666–1720), who developed great affection for Emanuel and left him a significant inheritance. His father, a Lutheran clergyman, later became a celebrated and controversial bishop, whose diocese included the Swedish churches in Pennsylvania and in London, England.

After studying at the University of Uppsala (1699–1709), Emanuel journeyed to England, the Netherlands, France, and Germany (1710–1715) to study and work with leading scientists in western Europe. Upon his return he apprenticed as an engineer under the brilliant Swedish inventor Christopher Polhem (1661–1751). He gained favor with Sweden's King Charles XII (1682–1718), who gave him a salaried position as an overseer of Sweden's mining industry (1716–1747). Although Emanuel was engaged, he never married.

After the death of Charles XII, Emanuel was ennobled by Queen Ulrika Eleonora (1688–1741), and his last name was changed to Swedenborg (or Svedenborg). This change in status gave him a seat in the Swedish House of Nobles, where he remained an active participant in the Swedish government throughout his life.

A member of the Royal Swedish Academy of Sciences, he devoted himself to studies that culminated in a number of publications, most notably a comprehensive three-volume work on natural philosophy and metallurgy (1734) that brought him recognition across Europe as a scientist. After 1734 he redirected his research and publishing to a study of anatomy in search of the interface between the soul and body, making several significant discoveries in physiology.

From 1743 to 1745 he entered a transitional phase that resulted in a shift of his main focus from science to theology. Throughout the rest of his life he maintained that this shift was brought about by Jesus Christ, who appeared to him, called him to a new mission, and opened his perception to a permanent dual consciousness of this life and the life after death.

He devoted the last decades of his life to studying Scripture and publishing eighteen theological titles that draw on the Bible, reasoning, and his own spiritual experiences. These works present a Christian theology with unique perspectives on the nature of God, the spiritual world, the Bible, the human mind, and the path to salvation.

Swedenborg died in London on March 29, 1772 (Gregorian calendar), at the age of eighty-four.